HOW TO RAISE MONARCH BUTTERFLIES

Guiding Wings: A Practical Guide to Nurturing Monarch Butterflies"

John Jerry

TABLE OF CONTENTS

INTRODUCTION..7

Understanding Monarch Butterflies...................7

The Life Cycle of Monarchs............................12

Importance of Monarch Conservation..............16

Monarch Biology and Behavior......................20

Monarch Migration Patterns...........................24

Threats to Monarch Populations.....................27

CREATING A MONARCH HABITAT......................33

Selecting Suitable Plants for Monarchs............33

Designing a Butterfly-Friendly Garden...........39

Providing Shelter and Water Sources...............43

Maintaining a Sustainable Habitat...................47

Enhancing Habitat Connectivity in Urban Areas 52

SOURCING MONARCH EGGS AND CATERPILLARS. 55

Identifying Monarch Eggs in the Wild..............55

Building Relationships with Local Breeders... 58

Ethical Considerations in Collecting Eggs.......60

Ensuring Egg and Caterpillar Health...............63

Transporting Eggs and Caterpillars Safely......65

CARING FOR MONARCH EGGS AND CATERPILLARS...69

Creating an Indoor Rearing Setup.....................69

Providing Adequate Temperature and Humidity..72

Feeding Monarch Caterpillars Properly...........74

Monitoring Caterpillar Growth and Development...76

Addressing Common Caterpillar Health Issues.. 79

THE TRANSFORMATION: FROM CATERPILLAR TO CHRYSALIS..82

Recognizing Signs of Caterpillar Pupation......82

Understanding the Chrysalis Formation Process...85

Protecting Chrysalises from Predators and Pests...88

Documenting   Chrysalis Development...........91

Preparing for Butterfly Emergence....................94

SUPPORTING HEALTHY CHRYSALIS FORMATION 98

Optimal Conditions for Chrysalis Care.............98

Managing Environmental Factors Effectively.... 101

Troubleshooting Chrysalis Issues.................... 104

Enhancing Chrysalis Security Measures........ 107

Promoting Chrysalis Stability and Success... 109

WITNESSING THE MIRACLE: EMERGENCE OF THE BUTTERFLY..113
Observing Butterfly Emergence Behaviors.....113
Assisting Butterflies During Emergence........ 116
Allowing Butterflies to Dry and Harden Wings... 119
Releasing Butterflies Responsibly................... 122
Capturing Moments of Butterfly Freedom.....125

PROVIDING PROPER NUTRITION FOR ADULT MONARCHS.. 128
Creating Butterfly Feeding Stations.................131
Offering Nutritious Nectar Sources................. 134
Maintaining Feeding Stations Cleanliness.....137
Supplementing Adult Monarch Diets When Necessary... 140

ENSURING SAFE RELEASE AND MIGRATION... 144
Timing Releases for Optimal Migration Periods 144
Selecting Suitable Release Sites....................... 147
Releasing Butterflies with Care and Respect.150
Monitoring Released Butterflies in the Wild. 153
Contributing to Citizen Science Initiatives....156

ENGAGING IN MONARCH CONSERVATION EFFORTS..........160

Participating in Monarch Tagging Programs...... 160

Advocating for Monarch-Friendly Policies... 163

Supporting Monarch Habitat Restoration Projects................166

Educating Others About Monarch Conservation 170

Taking Action to Protect Monarchs for Future Generations................173

CONCLUSION: BECOMING A STEWARD OF MONARCH BUTTERFLIES................176

INTRODUCTION

Understanding Monarch Butterflies

Monarch butterflies (Danaus plexippus) are perhaps one of the most iconic and beloved species of butterflies in the world. Delicate and vibrant, they captivate both scientists and nature enthusiasts alike with their remarkable life cycle and migratory behavior. In this chapter, we delve into the fascinating world of monarch butterflies, exploring their life cycle, biology, behavior, migration patterns, and the challenges they face in the modern world.

1. The Life Cycle of Monarchs:

Monarchs undergo a remarkable transformation from egg to caterpillar to chrysalis to adult butterfly. Understanding each stage of their life cycle is essential for successfully raising and conserving them. From the moment a tiny egg is laid on a milkweed leaf to the emergence of a magnificent butterfly, each phase is filled with wonder and intrigue.

2. Importance of Monarch Conservation:

Monarch butterflies play a vital role in ecosystem health as pollinators and indicators of environmental quality. Their decline in recent years has raised concerns about the health of our ecosystems and the impact of human activities on wildlife populations. By understanding the importance of monarch conservation, we can take meaningful steps to protect these beautiful insects and the habitats they rely on.

3. Monarch Biology and Behavior:

Monarchs possess unique adaptations that enable them to thrive in diverse habitats across North America. Their distinctive orange and black wing patterns serve as a warning to potential predators, while their ability to migrate thousands of miles is a testament to their resilience and adaptability. Exploring the biology and behavior of monarchs provides insights into their remarkable survival strategies.

4. Monarch Migration Patterns:

One of the most awe-inspiring phenomena in the natural world is the monarch butterfly migration. Each year, millions of monarchs embark on an epic journey spanning thousands of miles from their breeding grounds in North America to overwintering sites in Mexico or California. Understanding the intricacies of monarch migration patterns is essential for conserving these iconic insects and the habitats they depend on.

5. Threats to Monarch Populations:

Despite their remarkable resilience, monarch butterflies face a myriad of threats, including habitat loss, climate change, pesticide use, and disease. These threats have contributed to significant declines in monarch populations in recent decades, highlighting the urgent need for conservation action. By identifying and addressing the challenges facing monarchs, we can work together to ensure their survival for future generations to admire and enjoy.

6. Monarch Habitat Requirements:

Monarch butterflies are highly dependent on milkweed plants (Asclepias spp.) for breeding and larval development. Understanding the specific habitat requirements of monarchs, including the types of milkweed and nectar plants they rely on, is crucial for creating and maintaining suitable habitats. By providing the necessary resources, we can support healthy monarch populations in our local communities.

7. Reproductive Behavior and Mating Strategies:

The reproductive behavior of monarch butterflies is a fascinating aspect of their biology. From courtship rituals to mate selection, monarchs employ various strategies to ensure successful breeding. Exploring the intricacies of their mating behavior provides valuable insights into their reproductive success and population dynamics.

8. Seasonal Variations in Monarch Populations:

Monarch populations exhibit seasonal fluctuations in response to changing environmental conditions and migration patterns. Understanding these variations, including population dynamics and demographic trends, is essential for assessing the health of monarch populations and implementing targeted conservation efforts. By monitoring seasonal changes in monarch populations, we can better understand their needs and vulnerabilities throughout the year.

9. Genetic Diversity and Population Structure:

Genetic diversity plays a crucial role in the long-term survival of monarch butterflies. Maintaining healthy levels of genetic variation within populations is essential for adaptation to changing environmental conditions and resistance to disease. Exploring the genetic diversity and population structure of monarchs provides valuable insights into their evolutionary history and conservation genetics.

10. Interactions with Other Species:

Monarch butterflies interact with a wide range of other species, including predators, parasites, and mutualistic partners. Understanding these ecological interactions, such as predator-prey dynamics and plant-insect relationships, is essential for predicting the impact of environmental changes on monarch populations. By studying the complex web of interactions involving monarch butterflies, we can gain a deeper appreciation for their ecological significance and interconnectedness within ecosystems.

The Life Cycle of Monarchs

The life cycle of monarch butterflies is a captivating journey filled with remarkable transformations and intricate stages. From the tiny egg to the magnificent adult butterfly, each phase plays a vital role in the survival and perpetuation of this iconic species.

The life cycle begins when a female monarch butterfly lays her eggs on the underside of milkweed leaves. Milkweed, the sole host plant for monarch caterpillars, provides essential nutrients and chemicals necessary for their development. The female monarch carefully selects a suitable milkweed plant, depositing a single egg on a tender leaf. These eggs are tiny, no larger than a pinhead, and are often laid in clusters, ensuring the survival of at least some offspring despite potential threats.

After a few days, the egg hatches, revealing a minuscule caterpillar no bigger than a grain of rice. These newly emerged larvae, or caterpillars, immediately begin to feed voraciously on the milkweed leaves, consuming large quantities of plant material to fuel their rapid growth. As they grow, the caterpillars undergo a series of molts, shedding their exoskeletons to accommodate their increasing size. Each instar, or stage between molts, is marked by distinct changes in appearance, including the development of characteristic black, yellow, and white stripes along the caterpillar's body.

After approximately two weeks of feeding and growth, the fully grown caterpillar enters the pupal stage, forming a chrysalis in which it will undergo metamorphosis. The transformation from caterpillar to chrysalis is a remarkable process, during which the caterpillar secretes a silk pad and attaches itself to a suitable surface, such as a branch or stem. Once securely anchored, the caterpillar sheds its outer skin for the final time, revealing the green, jewel-like chrysalis beneath.

Inside the chrysalis, profound changes are taking place as the caterpillar's body undergoes a complete reorganization. Tissues and organs are broken down and rebuilt, forming the intricate structures of the adult butterfly. This process, known as metamorphosis, typically takes around ten to fourteen days to complete, though the exact timing may vary depending on environmental conditions such as temperature and humidity.

Finally, after weeks of waiting, the fully formed butterfly emerges from the chrysalis, its wings soft and crumpled. Over the next few hours, the butterfly pumps fluid into its wings, causing them to expand and harden into their characteristic shape. Once its wings are fully extended and dry, the monarch is ready to take flight for the first time, embarking on its brief but spectacular adult life.

As an adult, the monarch's primary goal is to mate and reproduce, continuing the cycle of life. Adult monarchs feed primarily on nectar from a wide range of flowers, using their long proboscis to extract the sweet liquid. During the breeding season, males and females engage in elaborate courtship rituals, with males competing for the attention of potential mates through aerial displays and pheromone release.

After mating, the female monarch searches for suitable milkweed plants on which to lay her eggs, thus completing the cycle and ensuring the next generation's survival. Throughout their adult lifespan, monarch butterflies may travel thousands of miles, undertaking incredible migratory journeys between breeding and overwintering sites. This remarkable life cycle, characterized by its beauty and resilience, serves as a testament to the monarch butterfly's extraordinary adaptability and endurance in the face of environmental challenges.

Importance of Monarch Conservation

The importance of monarch conservation cannot be overstated, as these iconic butterflies play a vital role in ecosystem health, pollination, and cultural heritage. Monarchs are not only beautiful creatures but also serve as indicators of environmental quality and biodiversity.

Here are several key reasons why monarch conservation is crucial:

Pollination: Monarch butterflies, like many other pollinators, play a significant role in pollinating a wide variety of flowering plants. As they feed on nectar, monarchs inadvertently transfer pollen from one flower to another, facilitating plant reproduction and ensuring the production of fruits, seeds, and new plants. By supporting monarch populations, we help maintain healthy ecosystems and ensure the continuation of essential pollination services.

Biodiversity: Monarchs are a keystone species whose presence influences the abundance and diversity of other organisms within their ecosystems. By conserving monarch habitat, we protect not only the butterflies themselves but also the myriad of plant and animal species that rely on the same resources. Healthy monarch populations indicate the overall health and resilience of ecosystems, contributing to greater biodiversity and ecological stability.

Cultural Significance: Monarch butterflies hold cultural significance for many communities around the world. From indigenous traditions to modern conservation movements, monarchs are celebrated as symbols of beauty, transformation, and resilience. Their annual migration, spanning thousands of miles and multiple generations, has inspired awe and wonder for centuries, uniting people across borders and cultures in appreciation of the natural world.

Educational Value: Monarch conservation provides valuable opportunities for education and outreach, inspiring curiosity and stewardship among people of all ages. By learning about the life cycle, behavior, and ecological importance of monarch butterflies, individuals can develop a deeper connection to nature and a greater understanding of the interconnectedness of all living things. Conservation efforts involving monarchs often serve as catalysts for broader environmental awareness and action.

Ecosystem Services: Monarch butterflies contribute to the provision of essential ecosystem services, such as nutrient cycling, soil formation, and water purification. By supporting healthy monarch populations, we help maintain the functioning of ecosystems and the services they provide, benefiting human well-being and livelihoods. From agricultural productivity to freshwater availability, the health of our ecosystems depends on the presence of pollinators like monarchs.

Climate Resilience: Monarch conservation can contribute to climate resilience by preserving habitat connectivity and promoting landscape-scale restoration efforts. As climate change alters temperature and precipitation patterns, monarch butterflies may face new challenges in finding suitable breeding and overwintering habitats. By conserving diverse and resilient habitats, we can help monarch populations adapt to changing environmental conditions and thrive in the future.

Therefore, monarch conservation is essential for preserving biodiversity, ecosystem services, cultural heritage, and educational opportunities. By working together to protect monarch butterflies and their habitats, we can ensure a brighter future for these iconic insects and the ecosystems they inhabit. Whether through habitat restoration, public awareness campaigns, or policy advocacy, every effort to conserve monarchs contributes to the broader goal of safeguarding our natural world for future generations.

Monarch Biology and Behavior

Monarch butterflies, with their distinctive orange and black wings, are not only visually stunning but also fascinating creatures with unique biology and behavior. Understanding the intricacies of monarch biology and behavior is essential for appreciating their ecological significance and implementing effective conservation strategies.

Biology:

Monarch butterflies belong to the family Nymphalidae and the genus Danaus, with the species name being Danaus plexippus. Their scientific name reflects their regal appearance and widespread distribution. Monarchs are large butterflies, with wingspans ranging from 3.5 to 4 inches, and exhibit sexual dimorphism, with males typically being slightly larger than females.

One of the most remarkable features of monarch biology is their migration behavior. Monarchs undertake an annual migration spanning thousands of miles between their breeding grounds in North America and overwintering sites in Mexico or California. This migratory phenomenon involves multiple generations of butterflies, with each successive generation making its way northward in the spring and southward in the fall.

Monarchs are also well-known for their reliance on milkweed plants (Asclepias spp.) as their sole host plant for breeding and larval development. The relationship between monarchs and milkweed is crucial to their survival, as milkweed provides essential nutrients and chemicals necessary for the development of monarch caterpillars. Monarchs have evolved to sequester toxins from milkweed, making them unpalatable to predators and contributing to their distinctive warning coloration.

Behavior:
Monarch butterflies exhibit a wide range of behaviors that are essential for their survival and reproduction. One of the most notable behaviors is their migratory journey, during which monarchs navigate using a combination of environmental cues, including the position of the sun,

magnetic fields, and landmarks. This remarkable navigational ability allows monarchs to travel thousands of miles with remarkable accuracy.

During the breeding season, monarchs engage in courtship rituals involving aerial displays and pheromone release to attract potential mates. Males actively patrol territories in search of females, while females carefully select suitable egg-laying sites on milkweed plants. After mating, females lay their eggs singly on the undersides of milkweed leaves, ensuring that each caterpillar has access to an ample food supply.

Once hatched, monarch caterpillars feed voraciously on milkweed leaves, undergoing rapid growth and development through a series of molts. As they grow, they exhibit distinct behavioral patterns, including leaf-shredding and frass deposition, which help regulate their environment and minimize predation risk. After completing their larval stage, monarch caterpillars undergo metamorphosis, forming chrysalises in which they undergo profound physiological changes before emerging as adult butterflies.

Throughout their adult lifespan, monarch butterflies engage in behaviors such as nectaring, basking, and mating, all of which are essential for their survival and reproduction. Monarchs also exhibit territorial behavior, with males defending prime nectaring sites and breeding territories from competitors. Additionally, monarchs play an important role in pollination, visiting a wide variety of flowers to feed on nectar and inadvertently transferring pollen between plants.

In addition, monarch butterflies possess a wealth of biological adaptations and behavioral strategies that enable them to thrive in diverse habitats and undertake extraordinary migratory journeys. By understanding the intricacies of monarch biology and behavior, we can better appreciate their ecological significance and implement effective conservation measures to ensure their survival for future generations to admire and enjoy.

Monarch Migration Patterns

Monarch migration patterns are among the most awe-inspiring phenomena in the natural world, captivating scientists and nature enthusiasts alike with their remarkable scope and complexity. Each year, millions of monarch butterflies embark on an epic journey spanning thousands of miles from their breeding grounds in North America to overwintering sites in Mexico or California. Understanding the intricacies of monarch migration patterns is essential for conserving these iconic insects and the habitats they depend on.

The monarch migration begins in late summer or early fall, as monarchs in North America prepare for their long journey southward. As days grow shorter and temperatures drop, a new generation of monarchs emerges from their chrysalises and begins the journey south. These monarchs are genetically programmed to orient themselves in a southwesterly direction, using a combination of environmental cues, including the position of the sun, magnetic fields, and landmarks, to guide their migration.

The first leg of the monarch migration takes monarchs from their breeding grounds in the United States and Canada to their overwintering sites in Mexico or California. Along the way, monarchs traverse vast distances, navigating over mountains, rivers, and other geographical barriers. Despite their delicate appearance, monarchs are remarkably resilient flyers, capable of covering up to 50 to 100 miles per day on their journey southward.

Upon reaching their overwintering sites, monarchs congregate in dense clusters in oyamel fir forests in the mountains of central Mexico or coastal groves in California. These overwintering sites provide monarchs with shelter from harsh weather conditions and protection from predators. The sight of millions of monarch butterflies blanketing the trees is a breathtaking spectacle, drawing visitors from around the world to witness this natural wonder.

In the spring, as temperatures begin to warm and days grow longer, monarchs prepare to resume their journey northward. As the first signs of spring emerge, monarchs become restless, and their behavior shifts from clustering to dispersal. With the onset of favorable weather conditions, monarchs begin their northward migration, returning to their breeding grounds in search of milkweed plants on which to lay their eggs.

The journey northward is a critical phase in the monarch migration cycle, as it marks the beginning of a new breeding season and the continuation of the monarch life cycle. Along the way, monarchs mate, feed, and lay eggs, initiating the next generation of monarch butterflies. As the cycle repeats itself, successive generations of monarchs continue the journey northward, each playing a vital role in maintaining the continuity of the migration.

Throughout their migration, monarchs face a myriad of challenges, including habitat loss, climate change, pesticide use, and natural disasters. These threats have contributed to significant declines in monarch populations in recent years, raising concerns about the long-term viability of the migration. Conservation efforts aimed at protecting monarch habitat, reducing pesticide use, and raising awareness about the importance of monarch butterflies are essential for ensuring the survival of this iconic species and the continuation of their remarkable migration. By working together to address these challenges, we can help monarchs thrive for generations to come and preserve one of the world's most remarkable natural wonders.

Threats to Monarch Populations

Threats to monarch populations pose significant challenges to the long-term survival of these iconic butterflies, which play a vital role in ecosystem health, pollination, and cultural heritage. Despite their remarkable resilience and adaptability, monarchs face a myriad of human-induced and natural threats that endanger their populations and disrupt their migratory cycles. Understanding these threats is essential for implementing effective conservation strategies and ensuring the continued existence of monarch butterflies.

Habitat Loss and Degradation:

Perhaps the most significant threat to monarch populations is habitat loss and degradation, particularly the decline of milkweed plants (Asclepias spp.), which serve as the sole host plant for monarch caterpillars. Urbanization, agricultural expansion, deforestation, and land development have led to the loss of millions of acres of milkweed habitat across North America, depriving monarchs of essential breeding and feeding grounds. Without access to suitable milkweed habitat, monarchs struggle to reproduce and sustain healthy populations, leading to declines in overall numbers.

Climate Change:

Climate change poses a significant threat to monarch populations by altering temperature and precipitation patterns, disrupting migratory cues, and impacting habitat suitability. Rising temperatures, extreme weather events, and shifting seasonal patterns can disrupt the delicate balance of monarch ecosystems, affecting butterfly behavior, plant phenology, and food availability. Changes in climate may also influence the timing and success of monarch migration, leading to mismatches between butterfly emergence and the availability of nectar sources or breeding habitat.

Pesticide Use:

The widespread use of pesticides, particularly herbicides and insecticides, poses a direct threat to monarch populations by contaminating milkweed plants and nectar sources and poisoning butterflies at various life stages. Herbicides used to control weeds in agricultural fields and roadside habitats can eliminate milkweed plants, depriving monarchs of essential breeding habitat. Insecticides used to control pest insects can also harm non-target species, including monarch caterpillars and adults, leading to population declines and reproductive failure.

Disease and Parasites:

Monarch butterflies are susceptible to a range of diseases and parasites that can impact individual fitness and population dynamics. One of the most well-known diseases affecting monarchs is Ophryocystis elektroscirrha (OE), a protozoan parasite that infects caterpillars and adult butterflies. Infected monarchs may exhibit reduced reproductive success, impaired flight ability, and increased susceptibility to predation. Additionally, monarchs face threats from other pathogens, parasites, and microbial agents that can weaken their immune systems and decrease overall population health.

Illegal Logging and Deforestation:

In the overwintering sites of central Mexico, monarch butterflies face threats from illegal logging and deforestation, which degrade and destroy their critical overwintering habitat. Despite conservation efforts to protect these areas, illegal logging continues to pose a significant threat to monarch populations, particularly in remote and inaccessible regions. Loss of habitat in the overwintering sites can disrupt monarch clustering behavior, expose butterflies to harsh weather conditions, and increase susceptibility to predation and disturbance.

Fragmentation and Habitat Fragmentation:

Habitat fragmentation, caused by the fragmentation of natural landscapes into smaller, isolated patches, can limit monarch dispersal and migration, reduce genetic diversity, and increase vulnerability to environmental stressors. Fragmented habitats may lack connectivity between breeding, feeding, and overwintering sites, making it difficult for monarchs to complete their life cycle and maintain healthy populations. Fragmentation also increases the risk of local extinctions and reduces the resilience of monarch ecosystems to environmental change.

Therefore, monarch populations face a wide range of threats that jeopardize their long-term survival and disrupt their remarkable migratory cycles. Addressing these threats requires concerted efforts from governments, conservation organizations, farmers, landowners, and individuals to protect and restore monarch habitat, reduce pesticide use, mitigate climate change impacts, and promote sustainable land management practices. By working together to address these challenges, we can ensure the continued existence of monarch butterflies and preserve their invaluable contributions to biodiversity, ecosystem function, and cultural heritage.

CREATING A MONARCH HABITAT

Selecting Suitable Plants for Monarchs

Selecting suitable plants for monarch butterflies is essential for creating and maintaining habitat that supports all stages of their life cycle. Monarchs rely on specific plant species, particularly milkweed (Asclepias spp.), as their sole host plant for breeding and larval development. By choosing the right plants for your garden or landscape, you can provide essential resources for monarchs and contribute to their conservation efforts.

Importance of Milkweed:
Milkweed plants are the cornerstone of monarch habitat, providing monarch caterpillars with essential nutrients and chemicals necessary for their growth and development. As the sole host plant for monarchs,

milkweed serves as the primary food source for monarch caterpillars, supplying them with proteins, fats, and toxins that make them unpalatable to predators. Without access to milkweed, monarchs cannot complete their life cycle, resulting in population declines and reproductive failure.

There are over 100 species of milkweed native to North America, each with its unique characteristics and growing requirements. Common milkweed (Asclepias syriaca), swamp milkweed (Asclepias incarnata), butterfly milkweed (Asclepias tuberosa), and tropical milkweed (Asclepias curassavica) are among the most popular species cultivated for monarch habitat restoration and gardening.

Native vs. Non-Native Milkweed:

When selecting milkweed plants for monarch habitat, it is essential to prioritize native species over non-native varieties. Native milkweed species have co-evolved with monarch butterflies and are well-adapted to local climate and soil conditions. They also provide higher-quality nectar and are less likely to harbor pathogens or parasites that can harm monarch populations.

In contrast, non-native milkweed species, such as tropical milkweed (Asclepias curassavica), may not provide the same level of support for monarchs and can potentially disrupt their migratory behavior. Tropical milkweed, in particular, has been associated with increased transmission of the protozoan parasite Ophryocystis elektroscirrha (OE) and delayed migration in monarch populations. Therefore, it is recommended to prioritize native milkweed species in monarch habitat restoration projects and garden plantings.

Diversity of Nectar Plants:

In addition to milkweed, monarch butterflies require a diverse array of nectar plants to sustain them throughout their adult life stage. Nectar plants provide monarchs with the energy and resources they need for flight, mating, and reproduction. When selecting nectar plants for monarch habitat, it is essential to choose species that bloom at different times of the year and provide a continuous source of nectar throughout the growing season.

Native wildflowers, such as purple coneflower (Echinacea purpurea), black-eyed Susan (Rudbeckia hirta), blazing star (Liatris spp.), and goldenrod (Solidago spp.), are excellent choices for attracting monarchs and other pollinators to your garden or landscape. By planting a diverse mix of nectar plants, you can create a vibrant and resilient habitat that supports a wide range of native pollinators and beneficial insects.

Considerations for Planting:

When planning your monarch habitat garden, consider factors such as soil type, sunlight exposure, and water availability to ensure the success of your plantings. Milkweed and nectar plants have specific growing requirements and may thrive in different environmental conditions.

Milkweed species, for example, prefer well-drained soils with full sun exposure, though some species, such as swamp milkweed, can tolerate partial shade and moist soils. Nectar plants may have varying soil and sunlight preferences, so it's essential to research each species' specific needs before planting.

Planting native plants is also beneficial for supporting local wildlife and promoting ecosystem resilience. Native plants have co-evolved with native insects, birds, and other wildlife, providing essential habitat and food sources for local biodiversity. By incorporating native plants into your monarch habitat garden, you can create a more sustainable and ecologically diverse landscape.

Maintenance and Care:
Once established, monarch habitat gardens require ongoing maintenance and care to ensure the health and vitality of the plants and the butterflies they support. Regular watering, mulching, and weeding can help maintain soil moisture and prevent competition from invasive species. Removing spent flowers and deadheading can promote continuous blooming and prolong the availability of nectar for monarchs and other pollinators.

Avoid the use of pesticides and herbicides in your monarch habitat garden, as these chemicals can harm monarchs and other beneficial insects. Instead, opt for organic gardening practices, such as companion planting, crop rotation, and natural pest control methods, to maintain a healthy and balanced ecosystem.

selecting suitable plants for monarchs is a critical step in creating habitat that supports all stages of their life cycle. By prioritizing native milkweed species, diversifying nectar plantings, and considering factors such as soil type and sunlight exposure, you can create a vibrant and resilient monarch habitat garden that attracts and sustains these iconic butterflies. With proper planning, maintenance, and care, you can make a meaningful contribution to monarch conservation efforts and help ensure the continued survival of these magnificent insects for generations to come.

Designing a Butterfly-Friendly Garden

Designing a butterfly-friendly garden tailored specifically for monarch butterflies is a rewarding endeavor that not only enhances the beauty of your outdoor space but also contributes to the conservation of these iconic insects. By creating a welcoming habitat that meets the specific needs of monarchs at all stages of their life cycle, you can attract these magnificent butterflies and support their populations for generations to come.

Incorporate Milkweed Plants:

The cornerstone of any monarch-friendly garden is the inclusion of milkweed plants (Asclepias spp.), which serve as the sole host plant for monarch caterpillars. Monarchs rely on milkweed for breeding and larval development, as the leaves provide essential nutrients and chemicals necessary for caterpillar growth. Incorporate a variety of native milkweed species into your garden, such as common milkweed (Asclepias syriaca), swamp milkweed (Asclepias incarnata), butterfly milkweed (Asclepias tuberosa), and tropical milkweed (Asclepias curassavica), to ensure a continuous supply of food for monarch caterpillars.

Provide Nectar-Rich Flowers:

In addition to milkweed, monarch butterflies require a diverse array of nectar-rich flowers to sustain them throughout their adult life stage. Select native wildflowers and flowering plants that bloom at different times of the year to provide a continuous source of nectar from spring through fall. Consider planting species such as purple coneflower (Echinacea purpurea), black-eyed Susan (Rudbeckia hirta), blazing star (Liatris spp.), goldenrod (Solidago spp.), and aster (Symphyotrichum spp.) to attract monarchs and other pollinators to your garden.

Create a Sunlit Habitat:

Monarch butterflies prefer sunny, open habitats with ample sunlight and shelter from strong winds. Design your garden to maximize sun exposure by selecting a location with southern or western exposure and minimizing shade from buildings, trees, and other structures. Provide sheltered areas, such as shrubs or trellises, where monarchs can rest and seek refuge from predators and adverse weather conditions.

Incorporate Host and Nectar Plant Groupings:
Arrange milkweed and nectar plants in clusters or groupings to create focal points and attract butterflies to specific areas of your garden. Planting in clusters mimics natural habitat conditions and makes it easier for monarchs to locate food and breeding sites. Consider planting milkweed near nectar sources to provide caterpillars with easy access to food as they emerge from their eggs and begin feeding.

Include Larval and Adult Butterfly Habitat:
In addition to milkweed and nectar plants, incorporate other elements into your garden to provide habitat for both monarch caterpillars and adult butterflies. Install butterfly-friendly features such as butterfly puddling stations, which provide essential minerals and moisture

for adult butterflies, and butterfly houses or shelters, where butterflies can roost and seek shelter from inclement weather.

Minimize Chemical Use:

Avoid the use of pesticides, herbicides, and other chemical inputs in your butterfly-friendly garden, as these substances can harm monarchs and other beneficial insects. Instead, opt for organic gardening practices, such as companion planting, crop rotation, and natural pest control methods, to maintain a healthy and balanced ecosystem. Choose disease-resistant plant varieties and practice proper garden sanitation to minimize the need for chemical interventions.

Provide Water Sources:

Offer shallow water sources, such as birdbaths, saucers filled with wet sand or gravel, or shallow dishes filled with water and rocks, to provide monarchs with access to moisture and minerals. Butterflies often congregate around puddles or damp areas to drink water and extract essential nutrients, particularly during hot, dry weather conditions.

Maintain Habitat Diversity:

Create a diverse and dynamic habitat by incorporating a variety of plant species, textures, colors, and heights into your garden design. Include native grasses, herbs, and groundcovers to provide additional habitat and forage for monarchs and other wildlife. Avoid monoculture plantings and strive to create a balanced and resilient ecosystem that supports a wide range of native plants and animals.

Providing Shelter and Water Sources

In a world where disparities persist, providing shelter and water sources emerges as a cornerstone of humanitarian efforts and sustainable development. The provision of these basic necessities goes beyond mere survival; it's about dignity, equity, and the foundation upon which thriving communities are built.

Shelter, more than just a roof over one's head, embodies safety, security, and belonging. Yet, millions around the globe are deprived of adequate housing, living in makeshift shelters susceptible to natural disasters, violence, and disease. Addressing this issue requires multifaceted approaches, from policy interventions to grassroots initiatives.

Governments play a pivotal role in enacting policies that ensure access to affordable housing for all citizens. Subsidized housing programs, zoning regulations, and incentives for affordable housing construction are some strategies employed to address housing inequalities. Additionally, investment in infrastructure such as roads, electricity, and sanitation facilities enhances the livability of communities and promotes economic development.

Non-governmental organizations (NGOs) and community-based organizations (CBOs) complement governmental efforts by providing direct assistance to vulnerable populations. Through initiatives like Habitat for Humanity, shelters are built or rehabilitated, empowering families to break the cycle of poverty and homelessness. Moreover, these organizations offer training and support to foster self-reliance among beneficiaries, creating sustainable solutions to housing challenges.

Simultaneously, ensuring access to clean water sources is paramount for public health and wellbeing. Despite progress in improving water access globally, disparities persist, with marginalized communities disproportionately affected by water scarcity and contamination. Addressing this issue requires holistic approaches that integrate infrastructure development, education, and community engagement.

Investments in water infrastructure, such as wells, boreholes, and piped water systems, are essential for expanding access to clean water sources. However, infrastructure alone is insufficient without concurrent efforts to promote hygiene practices and water conservation. Educational campaigns on water sanitation and hygiene (WASH) empower communities to safeguard their health and utilize water resources sustainably.

Furthermore, community participation and ownership are integral to the success and sustainability of water projects. Engaging local stakeholders in decision-making processes fosters a sense of ownership and responsibility, ensuring the long-term viability of water sources. Additionally, incorporating traditional knowledge and practices enhances the resilience of communities to environmental changes and water-related challenges.

Innovative solutions, such as rainwater harvesting and water purification technologies, offer promising avenues for addressing water scarcity in resource-constrained settings. By harnessing nature's resources and leveraging technological advancements, communities can mitigate the impacts of climate change and secure reliable water sources for future generations.

Ultimately, the provision of shelter and water sources is not just a matter of charity but a fundamental human right. Recognizing this, the international community has committed to achieving universal access to adequate housing and safe drinking water through initiatives like the Sustainable Development Goals (SDGs). By prioritizing these basic needs, we can build inclusive and resilient societies where every individual can thrive, regardless of their circumstances.

Maintaining a Sustainable Habitat

In an era marked by escalating environmental challenges, maintaining a sustainable habitat is imperative for the survival of both humanity and the planet. A sustainable habitat encompasses not only the physical environment but also the social, economic, and cultural aspects that contribute to human wellbeing and ecological balance. Achieving this equilibrium requires a concerted effort at local, national, and global levels, guided by principles of conservation, innovation, and collaboration.

At the heart of sustainable habitat management lies the preservation and restoration of natural ecosystems. These ecosystems provide essential services such as clean air, water purification, and climate regulation, upon which all life depends. Protecting biodiversity hotspots, conserving natural resources, and restoring degraded lands are central strategies for safeguarding ecosystem integrity.

Conservation efforts must be coupled with sustainable land use practices that prioritize ecological resilience and social equity. Adopting agroecological methods, promoting reforestation, and implementing sustainable forestry practices reduce deforestation, soil erosion, and habitat fragmentation while promoting biodiversity and supporting local livelihoods. Moreover, integrating traditional ecological knowledge with modern science enhances the effectiveness and cultural relevance of conservation initiatives.

Urban areas, home to over half of the world's population, play a crucial role in habitat sustainability. Sustainable urban planning and design principles emphasize compact, walkable cities with efficient public transportation systems, green spaces, and energy-efficient buildings. By reducing sprawl, minimizing resource consumption, and enhancing connectivity between urban and natural areas, cities can mitigate environmental impacts and enhance residents' quality of life.

Transitioning to renewable energy sources is paramount for mitigating climate change and reducing dependence on fossil fuels. Investments in solar, wind, hydro, and geothermal energy promote energy independence, stimulate economic growth, and mitigate greenhouse gas emissions. Furthermore, decentralized energy systems and microgrids increase resilience to power outages and natural disasters, ensuring uninterrupted access to electricity for all communities.

Water management is another critical aspect of sustaining habitat viability, particularly in the face of increasing water scarcity and pollution. Implementing water conservation measures, such as rainwater harvesting, greywater recycling, and efficient irrigation techniques, reduces water waste and enhances resilience to droughts. Additionally, restoring wetlands, protecting watersheds, and combating water pollution safeguard freshwater ecosystems and ensure access to clean water for all.

Promoting sustainable consumption and production patterns is essential for reducing resource depletion and environmental degradation. Embracing circular economy principles, such as recycling, upcycling, and waste minimization, closes resource loops and reduces reliance on finite resources. Moreover, fostering eco-friendly lifestyles through education, awareness campaigns, and green consumerism empowers individuals to make informed choices that benefit both themselves and the planet.

Collaboration among stakeholders is key to achieving sustainable habitat goals. Governments, businesses, civil society organizations, and local communities must work together to formulate and implement policies that balance environmental protection with economic development and social justice. Multilateral agreements, such as the Paris Agreement and the Convention on Biological Diversity, provide frameworks for international cooperation and collective action on pressing environmental issues.

Empowering marginalized communities, particularly indigenous peoples and local communities, is essential for sustainable habitat management. Recognizing their rights to land, resources, and self-determination not only upholds principles of justice and equity but also harnesses their traditional knowledge and stewardship practices for biodiversity conservation and ecosystem restoration.

In addition, maintaining a sustainable habitat requires a holistic approach that integrates environmental, social, economic, and cultural dimensions. By embracing conservation, innovation, and collaboration, we can create a world where humans and nature coexist in harmony, ensuring a prosperous and resilient future for generations to come.

Enhancing Habitat Connectivity in Urban Areas

In urban areas, habitat fragmentation poses a significant threat to biodiversity, leading to isolated pockets of green spaces and hindering the movement of wildlife. Enhancing habitat connectivity is crucial for promoting ecological resilience, supporting healthy ecosystems, and improving urban livability.

One effective strategy for enhancing habitat connectivity in urban areas is the creation of green corridors or wildlife corridors. These corridors serve as pathways linking fragmented habitats, allowing wildlife to move freely between them. By preserving or restoring green spaces such as parks, wetlands, and riparian zones and connecting them through green corridors, urban planners can create continuous habitat networks that support diverse species and ecological processes.

Furthermore, incorporating wildlife-friendly infrastructure into urban design promotes habitat connectivity while minimizing human-wildlife conflicts. Features such as wildlife overpasses, underpasses, and culverts allow animals to safely traverse roads, railways, and other barriers, reducing the risk of collisions and habitat fragmentation. Additionally, green roofs, vertical gardens, and green walls provide habitat and foraging opportunities for birds, insects, and other wildlife within urban built environments.

Community involvement and education are essential for successful habitat connectivity initiatives in urban areas. Engaging residents in habitat restoration projects, citizen science initiatives, and green space stewardship fosters a sense of ownership and appreciation for local biodiversity. Moreover, raising awareness about the importance of habitat connectivity and its benefits for both humans and wildlife encourages support for conservation efforts and promotes sustainable urban development practices.

Ultimately, enhancing habitat connectivity in urban areas is essential for promoting biodiversity conservation, ecological resilience, and human wellbeing. By incorporating green corridors, wildlife-friendly infrastructure, and community engagement into urban planning and design, cities can create interconnected networks of green spaces that support thriving ecosystems and enhance urban livability for residents and wildlife alike.

SOURCING MONARCH EGGS AND CATERPILLARS

Identifying Monarch Eggs in the Wild

Identifying Monarch eggs in the wild is a rewarding skill that allows enthusiasts and conservationists to contribute to the preservation of these iconic butterflies. Monarchs, known for their distinctive orange and black wings, undergo a remarkable metamorphosis, starting as tiny eggs laid on milkweed plants. Here's how to identify Monarch eggs in their natural habitat.

Firstly, knowing the preferred habitat of Monarchs is crucial. Monarchs lay their eggs exclusively on milkweed plants, as they are the sole host plants for their caterpillars. Milkweed species vary across regions, so familiarize yourself with the types native to your area.

Look for milkweed patches in fields, meadows, along roadsides, and in gardens.

Once you've located milkweed plants, carefully inspect the undersides of leaves, as Monarch butterflies typically lay their eggs there. Monarch eggs are small, about the size of a pinhead, and typically cylindrical or oval-shaped. They are pale green or yellow, with vertical ridges running along the length of the egg.

When identifying Monarch eggs, it's essential to distinguish them from similar-looking objects, such as insect frass (excrement) or fungal growths. Monarch eggs have a distinct shape and coloration, and they are typically laid singly, rather than in clusters like some insect eggs.

A magnifying glass or macro lens can be helpful for close inspection, especially if you're new to egg identification. Take your time and examine each milkweed leaf carefully, as Monarch eggs may be hidden among the foliage.

Once you've identified Monarch eggs, document their location and monitor them regularly for signs of hatching. After about 3-5 days, the eggs will darken in color, indicating that the caterpillars inside are ready to emerge. Witnessing this transformation firsthand is a remarkable experience and a testament to the beauty and resilience of nature.

By honing your skills in identifying Monarch eggs, you can contribute valuable data to citizen science projects and conservation efforts aimed at protecting Monarch populations and their habitat. Whether you're a casual observer or a dedicated conservationist, every egg spotted in the wild is a step towards ensuring the survival of these magnificent butterflies for generations to come.

Building Relationships with Local Breeders

Building relationships with local breeders is essential for anyone interested in animal husbandry, whether for personal enjoyment or professional endeavors. Local breeders offer valuable expertise, support, and resources that can enhance your breeding practices and contribute to the welfare of the animals involved.

First and foremost, fostering open communication with local breeders creates a network for sharing knowledge and experiences. Whether you're new to breeding or a seasoned enthusiast, connecting with breeders in your community allows you to exchange ideas, seek advice, and learn from each other's successes and challenges.

Moreover, building relationships with local breeders can provide access to high-quality breeding stock and genetic diversity. Breeders often specialize in specific breeds or species, and by establishing rapport with them, you may gain access to superior breeding lines, rare breeds, or unique traits that can improve the health, vigor, and conformation of your animals.

Additionally, collaborating with local breeders promotes ethical breeding practices and animal welfare standards. By working together to uphold responsible breeding practices, such as proper care, husbandry, and genetic selection, breeders can collectively contribute to the well-being of the animals they raise and ensure the long-term sustainability of their respective breeds or species.

Furthermore, supporting local breeders strengthens the community and local economy. By purchasing animals, supplies, or services from local breeders, you not only invest in the livelihoods of fellow enthusiasts but also contribute to the preservation of traditional breeding practices and heritage breeds.

So therefore, building relationships with local breeders is mutually beneficial, fostering a sense of camaraderie, promoting ethical breeding practices, and enhancing the quality and diversity of breeding stock. Whether you're seeking advice, sourcing animals, or simply connecting with like-minded individuals, investing in relationships with local breeders enriches the breeding experience and strengthens the bonds within the breeding community.

Ethical Considerations in Collecting Eggs

Ethical considerations in collecting eggs, whether from poultry, reptiles, or other animals, are paramount to ensuring the welfare and conservation of the animals involved. Collecting eggs can have implications for the reproductive success, genetic diversity, and population dynamics of the species, making it essential to approach egg collection with careful consideration and respect for the animals and their habitats.

First and foremost, it's crucial to prioritize the welfare of the animals when collecting eggs. This includes ensuring that egg collection practices do not cause undue stress or harm to the parent animals or their offspring. Minimizing disturbance to nesting sites, handling eggs with care to avoid damage, and providing appropriate environmental conditions for incubation are all essential aspects of ethical egg collection.

Furthermore, understanding the reproductive biology and natural history of the species is essential for making informed decisions about egg collection. Some species may be more sensitive to disturbance during nesting season, while others may require specific conditions for successful incubation. By respecting the natural behaviors and needs of the animals, collectors can minimize the impact of egg collection on wild populations.

Conservation considerations also play a significant role in ethical egg collection practices. For endangered or threatened species, collecting eggs for captive breeding or reintroduction programs may be necessary for population recovery efforts. However, such activities must be carefully managed to ensure that they do not harm wild populations or exacerbate existing threats to the species.

Transparency and accountability are essential aspects of ethical egg collection. Collectors should be transparent about their intentions and methods, seeking permits or permissions when required and adhering to relevant laws and regulations governing wildlife conservation and animal welfare. Additionally, documenting the outcomes of egg collection efforts, including hatch rates, genetic diversity, and population trends, can inform future conservation strategies and ensure that egg collection practices are evidence-based and effective.

In conclusion, ethical considerations in collecting eggs revolve around prioritizing animal welfare, respecting natural behaviors and habitats, and supporting conservation efforts. By approaching egg collection with compassion, responsibility, and a commitment to conservation, collectors can contribute to the well-being of animals and the sustainability of wild populations for future generations.

Ensuring Egg and Caterpillar Health

Ensuring the health of eggs and caterpillars is crucial for successful breeding and conservation efforts, whether for raising butterflies, moths, or other insects. Several key factors contribute to the well-being of eggs and caterpillars, including proper husbandry, nutrition, and environmental conditions.

Firstly, maintaining optimal conditions for egg laying and incubation is essential for egg health. Providing clean, suitable substrate or nesting materials, such as leaves or soil, ensures a safe and conducive environment for egg deposition. Monitoring temperature and humidity levels, as well as minimizing disturbance to nesting sites, helps promote successful egg development and hatching.

Once eggs hatch and caterpillars emerge, providing a nutritious diet is essential for their growth and development. For example, if raising butterfly caterpillars, ensuring a constant supply of their host plant is crucial, as it provides essential nutrients and sustains their growth. Monitoring caterpillar feeding behavior and providing fresh food regularly help prevent nutritional deficiencies and promote healthy growth.

Furthermore, maintaining a clean and hygienic rearing environment is essential for preventing disease and parasitism. Regularly cleaning rearing containers, removing frass (caterpillar waste), and monitoring for signs of illness or parasites help minimize the risk of infection and ensure the overall health of the caterpillars.

Finally, paying attention to environmental factors such as temperature, humidity, and light exposure is crucial for caterpillar health. Caterpillars have specific environmental requirements at different stages of their development, and providing suitable conditions helps support their physiological processes and immune function.

Nevertheless, ensuring the health of eggs and caterpillars requires attention to various factors, including proper husbandry practices, nutrition, hygiene, and environmental conditions. By providing a supportive and nurturing environment, breeders and conservationists can contribute to the well-being and success of these fascinating creatures and promote their conservation for future generations.

Transporting Eggs and Caterpillars Safely

Transporting eggs and caterpillars safely is essential for maintaining their health and well-being during transit, whether for breeding, research, or conservation purposes. Proper handling and preparation are crucial to minimize stress, prevent injury, and ensure the survival of these delicate creatures.

Firstly, it's important to use suitable containers for transporting eggs and caterpillars. Small, well-ventilated containers, such as plastic or mesh containers with lids, are ideal for preventing escape and providing adequate airflow. Ensure that the containers are clean and free from any debris or contaminants that could harm the eggs or caterpillars.

When transporting eggs, it's essential to keep them secure and stable to prevent damage. Use cushioning materials, such as tissue paper or soft padding, to protect the eggs from jostling or impact during transit. Place the eggs in a shallow, sturdy container lined with cushioning material, ensuring that they are not overcrowded and have room to breathe.

For transporting caterpillars, provide ample space and suitable substrate to prevent overcrowding and stress. Transfer the caterpillars to clean containers lined with fresh food or substrate, ensuring that they have enough space to move around and feed comfortably. Avoid overcrowding containers, as this can lead to competition for food and increased stress levels among the caterpillars.

Maintaining stable environmental conditions during transport is crucial for the health and safety of eggs and caterpillars. Monitor temperature, humidity, and airflow levels, and take steps to minimize fluctuations during transit. Avoid exposing the containers to extreme temperatures, direct sunlight, or drafts, as these can have detrimental effects on the eggs and caterpillars.

Additionally, handle eggs and caterpillars with care to prevent injury or stress. Use gentle movements and avoid shaking or disturbing the containers unnecessarily. If transporting caterpillars on host plants, secure the plants to prevent them from tipping over or becoming damaged during transit.

Ultimately, transporting eggs and caterpillars safely requires careful planning, proper containers, and attention to environmental conditions. By following these guidelines and taking precautions to minimize stress and ensure stability, breeders, researchers, and conservationists can transport these delicate creatures safely and effectively, supporting their health and well-being throughout the journey.

CARING FOR MONARCH EGGS AND CATERPILLARS

Creating an Indoor Rearing Setup

Creating an indoor rearing setup is essential for breeders, enthusiasts, and researchers looking to rear insects such as butterflies, moths, or other small creatures in a controlled environment. Whether for educational purposes, conservation efforts, or personal enjoyment, setting up an indoor rearing space requires careful planning and consideration of the needs of the animals being raised.

Firstly, choose an appropriate location for your indoor rearing setup. Select a well-ventilated area away from drafts, direct sunlight, and temperature fluctuations. A spare room, garage, or dedicated shelf space can serve as an ideal location for your rearing setup.

Next, gather the necessary supplies and equipment for your indoor rearing setup. This may include rearing containers, such as mesh or plastic containers with lids, suitable substrate or host plants for the insects, feeding dishes or containers, and cleaning supplies. Ensure that all materials are clean, sterilized, and free from contaminants that could harm the insects.

Once you have assembled your supplies, set up your rearing containers and prepare the substrate or host plants for the insects. Provide ample space and appropriate environmental conditions for the species you are rearing, including temperature, humidity, and lighting requirements. Monitor environmental conditions regularly and make adjustments as needed to maintain optimal conditions for the insects.

In addition to providing suitable housing and environmental conditions, it's essential to establish a feeding and cleaning routine for your indoor rearing setup. Depending on the species you are rearing, you may need to provide fresh food or substrate regularly, remove waste and debris from the containers, and clean the rearing setup to prevent disease and contamination.

Finally, monitor the health and behavior of the insects closely and respond promptly to any signs of stress, illness, or other issues. Regular observation and care are essential for ensuring the well-being and success of the insects in your indoor rearing setup.

Furthermore, creating an indoor rearing setup requires careful planning, attention to detail, and a commitment to providing a suitable environment for the insects being raised. By following these guidelines and providing appropriate housing, environmental conditions, and care, you can create a successful indoor rearing setup for rearing insects and supporting their health and well-being.

Providing Adequate Temperature and Humidity

Providing adequate temperature and humidity is essential for maintaining the health and well-being of various organisms, including plants, animals, and insects. Both temperature and humidity play critical roles in physiological processes, growth, reproduction, and overall vitality. Here's how to ensure optimal conditions for your living organisms:

Temperature regulation is crucial for organisms, as it influences metabolic rate, enzyme activity, and overall function. Different species have specific temperature requirements, so it's essential to research the ideal temperature range for the organisms you are caring for. Use thermometers to monitor temperature levels accurately and make adjustments as needed, using heating or cooling devices such as heat mats, heaters, fans, or air conditioning units to maintain the desired temperature range.

Humidity levels also significantly impact the health and well-being of organisms, particularly those from tropical or humid environments. High humidity levels help prevent dehydration, facilitate respiration, and support healthy skin or exoskeleton function. Conversely, low humidity can lead to desiccation, respiratory problems, or impaired growth. Use hygrometers to monitor humidity levels and provide appropriate humidity sources such as misting systems, humidifiers, or substrate moisture to maintain optimal conditions.

In addition to monitoring temperature and humidity levels, consider the environmental requirements and preferences of the organisms you are caring for. Some species may require specific temperature gradients or humidity fluctuations throughout the day or night, mimicking their natural habitat conditions. By understanding and meeting the temperature and humidity needs of your organisms, you can create a supportive and nurturing environment that promotes health, vitality, and overall well-being.

Feeding Monarch Caterpillars Properly

Feeding Monarch caterpillars properly is essential for their growth, development, and eventual transformation into butterflies. As specialized herbivores, Monarch caterpillars feed exclusively on milkweed plants (Asclepias spp.), making it crucial to provide a suitable and abundant food source to support their dietary needs.

Firstly, it's essential to choose healthy milkweed plants for feeding Monarch caterpillars. Select milkweed species native to your region, as they provide the most suitable nutrition and support for local Monarch populations. Avoid using milkweed plants treated with pesticides or herbicides, as these chemicals can be harmful or fatal to caterpillars.

Provide a variety of milkweed leaves to caterpillars at different stages of development, as they have specific preferences for younger, tender leaves or older, mature leaves. Harvest fresh milkweed leaves regularly, removing any damaged or wilted foliage, and rinse them thoroughly with water to remove contaminants before feeding them to the caterpillars.

Monitor caterpillar feeding behavior closely and replenish milkweed leaves as needed to ensure a constant food supply. Caterpillars consume large quantities of plant material to support their rapid growth, so it's essential to provide an ample food source to meet their nutritional needs.

In addition to providing milkweed leaves, consider supplementing the caterpillars' diet with artificial nectar sources, such as sugar water or honey water. These supplemental sources provide additional energy and hydration for the caterpillars, particularly during periods of high activity or environmental stress.

Avoid overcrowding caterpillars in feeding containers, as this can lead to competition for food and increased stress levels among the caterpillars. Provide ample space and suitable environmental conditions, such as proper ventilation and humidity levels, to support their health and well-being.

Finally, observe caterpillar behavior closely and monitor for signs of illness, stress, or nutritional deficiencies. Respond promptly to any issues by adjusting feeding practices, providing supplemental nutrition or hydration, or seeking veterinary advice if necessary.

By providing Monarch caterpillars with a suitable and abundant food source, you can support their growth and development and contribute to the conservation of these iconic butterflies for future generations to enjoy.

Monitoring Caterpillar Growth and Development

Monitoring caterpillar growth and development is essential for understanding their life cycle, identifying potential issues, and providing appropriate care to support their health and well-being.

Here's how to effectively monitor caterpillar growth and development:

1. Regular Observation: Spend time observing caterpillars daily to track their growth and behavior. Note changes in size, coloration, and activity levels as caterpillars progress through their developmental stages.

2. Measuring Size: Use a ruler or measuring tape to measure the length of caterpillars regularly. Record measurements to track growth rates and identify any abnormalities or deviations from expected growth patterns.

3. Recording Developmental Stage: Identify and record the developmental stage of caterpillars, such as instars (larval stages) or molts (shedding of the exoskeleton). Note any changes in body shape, color patterns, or behavior associated with each developmental stage.

4. Monitoring Feeding Behavior: Observe caterpillars' feeding behavior and appetite, ensuring they are actively consuming food and exhibiting healthy eating habits. Lack of appetite or reduced feeding activity may indicate stress, illness, or nutritional deficiencies.

5. Inspecting Feces (Frass): Examine caterpillar feces (frass) for color, consistency, and frequency of elimination. Healthy caterpillars produce firm, cylindrical frass regularly, while abnormal frass may indicate digestive issues or other health problems.

6. Documenting Environmental Conditions: Record environmental factors such as temperature, humidity, and lighting levels in the rearing environment. Monitor fluctuations in environmental conditions and their potential impact on caterpillar growth and development.

7. Seeking Veterinary Advice: If you observe any abnormalities, unusual behavior, or signs of illness in caterpillars, seek veterinary advice promptly. A veterinarian experienced in insect care can provide guidance on diagnosis, treatment, and preventive measures to support caterpillar health and well-being.

By consistently monitoring caterpillar growth and development, you can gain valuable insights into their life cycle and health status, enabling you to provide optimal care and support their successful transformation into butterflies or moths.

Addressing Common Caterpillar Health Issues

Addressing common caterpillar health issues is crucial for ensuring the well-being and success of these delicate creatures during rearing or observation. By recognizing and responding promptly to health issues, you can help caterpillars thrive and reach their full potential.

Here are some common caterpillar health issues and how to address them:

1. **Dehydration:** Caterpillars are susceptible to dehydration, especially in dry or low-humidity environments. Provide a moisture source such as damp paper towels, moistened cotton balls, or a shallow dish of water for caterpillars to drink from. Ensure that the moisture source is clean and replaced regularly to prevent contamination.

2. **Malnutrition:** Inadequate nutrition can lead to stunted growth, developmental abnormalities, and increased susceptibility to disease. Ensure caterpillars have access to a suitable and abundant food source, such as fresh milkweed leaves for Monarch caterpillars, and monitor feeding behavior to ensure they are consuming enough food.

3. **Parasites:** Caterpillars are vulnerable to parasitic infections from organisms such as parasitoid wasps, flies, or mites. Monitor caterpillars closely for signs of parasitism, such as unusual behavior, sluggishness, or the

presence of parasitic larvae or eggs on their bodies. Remove and isolate affected caterpillars promptly to prevent the spread of parasites to healthy individuals.

4. Bacterial or Fungal Infections: Poor hygiene, overcrowding, and environmental factors can contribute to bacterial or fungal infections in caterpillars. Keep rearing containers clean and dry, remove any contaminated substrate or food, and provide proper ventilation to reduce the risk of infection. If caterpillars show signs of illness, such as lethargy, loss of appetite, or visible lesions, isolate affected individuals and consult a veterinarian experienced in insect care for diagnosis and treatment options.

By addressing common caterpillar health issues proactively and providing appropriate care and support, you can promote the health and well-being of these fascinating creatures and contribute to their successful development into butterflies or moths.

THE TRANSFORMATION: FROM CATERPILLAR TO CHRYSALIS

Recognizing Signs of Caterpillar Pupation

Recognizing signs of caterpillar pupation is an exciting stage in the life cycle of butterflies and moths. Pupation marks the transition from the larval stage (caterpillar) to the adult stage (butterfly or moth) and involves dramatic physiological changes as the caterpillar undergoes metamorphosis within its protective cocoon or chrysalis.

Here are some key signs to look for when recognizing caterpillar pupation:

1. Decreased Feeding Activity: As caterpillars prepare for pupation, they often exhibit reduced feeding activity and may stop eating altogether. This decrease in appetite is a natural response as the caterpillar's body undergoes physiological changes in preparation for metamorphosis.

2. Wandering Behavior: Prior to pupation, caterpillars may become restless and exhibit wandering behavior, actively searching for a suitable pupation site. They may crawl away from their food source or rearing container in search of a sheltered, secure location to undergo metamorphosis.

3. Spinning Silk: Many caterpillar species spin silk to create a protective cocoon or chrysalis in which to pupate. Look for signs of silk spinning, such as the caterpillar weaving silk threads around itself or the surrounding environment. Silk may be visible as strands or patches on leaves, branches, or other surfaces near the caterpillar's location.

4. Formation of Pupal Structure: As caterpillars enter the pupation stage, they undergo physical changes to their body structure, including the formation of a pupal case or chrysalis. Depending on the species, pupal structures may vary in appearance, ranging from soft, silk-covered cocoons to hard, chitinous chrysalises.

5. Immobility: Once the caterpillar has formed its pupal structure, it becomes relatively immobile as it undergoes metamorphosis. The caterpillar may attach itself securely to the pupation site using silk threads or adhesive secretions, remaining motionless for several days or weeks until the transformation is complete.

By recognizing these signs of caterpillar pupation, observers can witness the remarkable process of metamorphosis and marvel at the beauty and complexity of nature's life cycles. Observing caterpillar pupation is a rewarding experience that provides valuable insights into the natural world and fosters a deeper appreciation for the wonders of insect biology.

Understanding the Chrysalis Formation Process

Understanding the chrysalis formation process is key to appreciating the remarkable transformation that caterpillars undergo as they transition into butterflies or moths. The formation of a chrysalis marks the beginning of metamorphosis, a complex series of physiological changes that culminate in the emergence of a fully-formed adult insect.

Here's a closer look at the stages involved in chrysalis formation:

1. Prepupal Stage: Before forming a chrysalis, the caterpillar enters a prepupal stage characterized by physiological changes in preparation for metamorphosis. During this stage, the caterpillar may exhibit wandering behavior, searching for a suitable pupation site.

2. Attachment: Once a suitable pupation site is found, the caterpillar attaches itself securely using silk threads or adhesive secretions. It may anchor itself to a leaf, stem, branch, or other surface using its terminal claspers or specialized hooks known as cremaster.

3. Spinning Silk: The caterpillar begins to spin silk threads around its body, forming a protective structure known as a pupal case or chrysalis. The silk may be produced from specialized glands located near the caterpillar's mouthparts or along its body.

4. Pupal Formation: As the caterpillar continues to spin silk, it undergoes physical changes to its body structure, including the formation of the pupal case or chrysalis. The chrysalis may vary in appearance depending on the species, ranging from soft and silk-covered to hard and chitinous.

5. Metamorphosis: Inside the chrysalis, the caterpillar undergoes metamorphosis, a remarkable process of cellular reorganization and tissue differentiation. During this stage, the caterpillar's body breaks down into a soupy substance known as imaginal discs, which gradually develop into the adult structures of the butterfly or moth.

6. Emergence: After several days or weeks of metamorphosis, the fully-formed adult insect emerges from the chrysalis. The emergence process, known as eclosion, typically occurs in the early morning hours and may take several minutes to complete as the adult insect expands and dries its wings.

Understanding the chrysalis formation process provides insight into the intricate and awe-inspiring journey of caterpillars as they undergo metamorphosis. Witnessing the emergence of a butterfly or moth from its chrysalis is a testament to the beauty and wonder of nature's life cycles.

Protecting Chrysalises from Predators and Pests

Protecting chrysalises from predators and pests is crucial for ensuring the successful development and emergence of butterflies and moths. Chrysalises are vulnerable to predation, parasitism, and damage from various natural enemies, making it essential to take proactive measures to safeguard them during the pupation stage.

Here are some strategies for protecting chrysalises from predators and pests:

1. Choose Safe Pupation Sites: Selecting safe pupation sites can help minimize the risk of predation and parasitism. Choose locations that are sheltered, hidden, and inaccessible to potential predators, such as under leaves, within dense vegetation, or on elevated surfaces out of reach of ground-dwelling predators.

2. Use Protective Enclosures: Install protective enclosures or netting around chrysalises to create a physical barrier against predators and pests. Mesh netting or fabric sleeves can be placed around pupation sites to deter birds, insects, and other animals from accessing the chrysalises.

3. Monitor and Remove Predators: Regularly monitor chrysalis sites for signs of predation or pest activity, such as chew marks, holes, or damage to the pupal case. Remove any predators or pests found near chrysalises, such as spiders, ants, or parasitic wasps, to prevent them from harming the developing pupae.

4. Provide Natural Predators: Introduce natural predators of pest species to the environment to help control pest populations and reduce the risk of damage to chrysalises. For example, releasing predatory insects such as ladybugs or lacewings can help control aphids, caterpillars, and other pest species that may pose a threat to chrysalises.

5. Maintain Cleanliness: Keep pupation sites clean and free from debris, detritus, and organic matter that may attract pests or provide hiding places for predators.

Regularly remove fallen leaves, plant debris, and other potential sources of food or shelter for pests and predators.

6. Avoid Pesticides: Refrain from using chemical pesticides or insecticides near chrysalis sites, as these may inadvertently harm developing pupae or disrupt natural predator-prey relationships. Instead, rely on non-toxic pest management methods, such as biological control or cultural practices, to minimize pest damage without harming chrysalises or other beneficial organisms.

By implementing these strategies for protecting chrysalises from predators and pests, you can help ensure the successful development and emergence of butterflies and moths, contributing to their conservation and survival in the wild.

Documenting Chrysalis Development

Documenting chrysalis development is a valuable and rewarding activity that allows observers to gain insights into the remarkable process of metamorphosis and contribute to scientific knowledge and understanding. By carefully documenting the stages of chrysalis development, observers can track changes over time, observe key milestones, and gain a deeper appreciation for the intricacies of butterfly and moth biology.

Here are some tips for documenting chrysalis development effectively:

1. Photography: Use a high-quality camera or smartphone with macro capabilities to capture detailed images of the chrysalis at various stages of development. Photograph the chrysalis from multiple angles, focusing on key features such as coloration, texture, and shape.

2. Time-Lapse Photography: Consider setting up a time-lapse camera or recording device to capture the entire process of chrysalis development from start to finish. Time-lapse photography allows observers to document subtle changes and transformations that occur over hours, days, or weeks.

3. Note-taking: Keep detailed notes on observations, including dates, times, and environmental conditions such as temperature, humidity, and lighting. Note any changes in the chrysalis's appearance, behavior, or posture, as well as any significant events such as molting or emergence.

4. Journaling: Maintain a journal or diary to record personal observations, thoughts, and reflections on the process of chrysalis development. Documenting your experiences and emotions can add depth and meaning to the observation process and provide valuable insights into your own learning and growth as an observer.

5. Video Documentation: Record videos of the chrysalis at different stages of development, capturing movements, behaviors, and interactions with the surrounding environment. Videos can provide a dynamic and immersive perspective on chrysalis development and allow observers to share their experiences with others.

6. Data Collection: Collect quantitative data on chrysalis development, such as measurements of size, weight, or coloration, to track changes over time and analyze patterns or trends. Quantitative data can enhance the scientific rigor of your observations and contribute to broader research efforts on butterfly and moth biology.

By documenting chrysalis development thoughtfully and systematically, observers can contribute valuable information to our understanding of butterfly and moth life cycles, behavior, and ecology. Whether for personal enjoyment, educational purposes, or scientific research, documenting chrysalis development offers a unique opportunity to connect with nature and contribute to the ongoing exploration of the natural world.

Preparing for Butterfly Emergence

Preparing for butterfly emergence is an exciting and crucial stage in the process of rearing butterflies or observing them in their natural habitat. Proper preparation ensures that butterflies emerge safely and are provided with the necessary support for their transition to adulthood.

Here are some essential steps for preparing for butterfly emergence:

1. Monitoring Chrysalises: Monitor chrysalises closely for signs of impending emergence, such as darkening or transparency of the pupal case, changes in posture, or visible movement within the chrysalis. Observers should be vigilant and attentive to catch the moment when butterflies begin to emerge.

2. Creating Emergence Chambers: Prepare emergence chambers or enclosures to provide a safe and controlled environment for butterflies to emerge. Use mesh cages or netted enclosures with ample space for butterflies to stretch and expand their wings after emergence.

3.Providing Suitable Perches: Place natural or artificial perches inside the emergence chamber to provide butterflies with a stable surface to cling to during emergence. Perches should be positioned at different heights and angles to accommodate butterflies of various sizes and species.

4. Maintaining Optimal Environmental Conditions: Ensure that environmental conditions within the emergence chamber are conducive to butterfly emergence and development. Monitor temperature, humidity, and lighting levels, and make adjustments as needed to create a comfortable and supportive environment for butterflies.

5. Preparing Food and Nectar Sources: Provide freshly cut flowers or artificial nectar sources inside the emergence chamber to nourish butterflies after emergence. Ensure that food sources are free from pesticides, contaminants, or other harmful substances that could harm butterflies.

6. Observing and Assisting Emergence: Once butterflies begin to emerge, observe the process closely and be prepared to assist if needed. Some butterflies may require assistance in breaking free from their pupal case or spreading their wings properly after emergence. Use caution and gentle handling to avoid causing injury or stress to emerging butterflies.

7. Releasing Butterflies: After butterflies have emerged and their wings have fully expanded and dried, release them into a suitable outdoor habitat. Choose a calm, sunny day with mild temperatures for optimal butterfly release conditions.

By following these steps and preparing carefully for butterfly emergence, observers can ensure a smooth and successful transition for butterflies from chrysalis to adulthood. Providing a supportive environment and attentive care during this critical stage helps promote the health and well-being of emerging butterflies and enhances the overall experience of witnessing their remarkable transformation.

SUPPORTING HEALTHY CHRYSALIS FORMATION

Optimal Conditions for Chrysalis Care

Optimal conditions for chrysalis care are essential for ensuring the successful development and emergence of butterflies and moths. Chrysalises are delicate structures that require specific environmental conditions to support metamorphosis and facilitate the transformation from pupa to adult insect.

Here are some key factors to consider when providing optimal conditions for chrysalis care:

1. Stable Temperature: Maintain a stable temperature within the chrysalis care environment to support consistent development and metabolic activity. Ideal temperatures vary depending on the species, but generally fall within the range of 70-85°F (21-29°C).

Avoid drastic temperature fluctuations, as they can disrupt chrysalis development and increase stress on emerging butterflies.

2. High Humidity: Provide high humidity levels to prevent desiccation and dehydration of chrysalises, which can lead to developmental abnormalities or failure to emerge. Aim for humidity levels of 60-80% to create a moist environment conducive to pupal development. Use misting systems, humidifiers, or moistened paper towels to maintain humidity levels within the chrysalis care enclosure.

3. Adequate Ventilation: Ensure proper ventilation within the chrysalis care enclosure to prevent the buildup of excess moisture and reduce the risk of fungal or bacterial growth. Use mesh cages or netted enclosures with breathable materials to allow for airflow while maintaining humidity levels. Monitor ventilation regularly and adjust as needed to maintain optimal conditions.

4. Low Light Intensity: Provide low light intensity within the chrysalis care environment to minimize stress on developing pupae and reduce the risk of premature emergence. Avoid exposing chrysalises to direct sunlight or bright artificial lighting, as excessive light can disrupt pupal development and cause abnormalities in emerging butterflies.

5. Cleanliness: Keep the chrysalis care enclosure clean and free from debris, detritus, and contaminants that could harm developing pupae or attract pests. Regularly remove fallen leaves, frass (caterpillar waste), and other organic matter, and clean surfaces with mild disinfectants to prevent the spread of pathogens.

By maintaining optimal conditions for chrysalis care, observers can support the health and well-being of developing pupae and ensure the successful emergence of butterflies and moths. Providing a stable environment with appropriate temperature, humidity, ventilation, and cleanliness promotes smooth metamorphosis and enhances the overall experience of witnessing the remarkable transformation of these fascinating insects.

Managing Environmental Factors Effectively

Managing environmental factors effectively is crucial for maintaining the health, well-being, and productivity of various organisms, including plants, animals, and insects. By understanding and controlling key environmental variables, observers can create optimal conditions for growth, development, and overall success.

__Here are some strategies for managing environmental factors effectively:__

1. **Temperature Control:** Monitor and regulate temperature levels to ensure they remain within the optimal range for the organisms being cared for. Use heating or cooling devices, such as heaters, fans, or air conditioning units, to maintain stable temperature

conditions in indoor or outdoor environments. Consider the temperature preferences of the organisms and make adjustments as needed to provide a comfortable and supportive environment.

2. Humidity Management: Maintain appropriate humidity levels to prevent dehydration or excessive moisture buildup, which can lead to health problems or stress in organisms. Use humidifiers, misting systems, or moisture-retaining substrates to adjust humidity levels as needed and create a suitable microclimate for the organisms.

3. Lighting Considerations: Provide adequate lighting for photosynthesis, growth, and behavioral rhythms in organisms that rely on light cues. Adjust lighting intensity, duration, and spectrum to mimic natural light cycles and meet the specific requirements of the organisms being cared for. Use artificial lighting sources, such as full-spectrum bulbs or LED grow lights, to supplement natural light in indoor environments.

4.Ventilation and Air Quality: Ensure proper ventilation to maintain air circulation and prevent the buildup of stagnant air, odors, or pollutants that can negatively impact organisms' health. Use fans, air purifiers, or natural ventilation methods to improve air quality and create a fresh and oxygen-rich environment for organisms.

5. Cleanliness and Hygiene: Keep the environment clean and free from contaminants, debris, and pathogens that could harm organisms or interfere with their growth and development. Establish regular cleaning and maintenance routines to remove waste, sterilize equipment, and prevent the spread of disease or pests.

By effectively managing environmental factors, observers can create optimal conditions for the organisms they care for, promoting health, well-being, and productivity. By understanding the unique environmental requirements of different organisms and implementing appropriate management strategies, observers can support their success and contribute to their overall welfare.

Troubleshooting Chrysalis Issues

Troubleshooting chrysalis issues is essential for ensuring the successful development and emergence of butterflies and moths. Chrysalises are vulnerable to various problems that can arise during the pupation process, including developmental abnormalities, infections, and environmental stressors.

Here are some common chrysalis issues and how to address them effectively:

1. **Deformation or Abnormalities:** If a chrysalis appears misshapen, discolored, or exhibits other abnormalities, it may indicate developmental issues or physical damage. Assess the chrysalis carefully and determine the cause of the deformation. If the issue is minor, such as a slight dent or crease, monitor the

chrysalis closely and provide supportive care to ensure successful emergence. If the deformity is severe or progressive, consider consulting a veterinarian or experienced entomologist for advice on potential interventions.

2. Disease or Infection: Chrysalises are susceptible to fungal, bacterial, or viral infections that can compromise their development and health. Look for signs of discoloration, mold growth, or unusual odor emanating from the chrysalis, which may indicate the presence of infection. If infection is suspected, isolate affected chrysalises and implement strict hygiene measures to prevent the spread of disease. Consider treating infected chrysalises with antifungal or antibacterial agents under the guidance of a professional.

3. Environmental Stress: Environmental factors such as temperature fluctuations, humidity levels, or inadequate ventilation can stress chrysalises and disrupt their development. Monitor environmental conditions closely and make adjustments as needed to create a stable and supportive environment for pupal development. Provide adequate temperature, humidity, and ventilation to minimize stress on chrysalises and promote successful emergence.

4. Predation or Damage: Chrysalises are vulnerable to predation by insects, birds, or other animals, as well as physical damage from handling or environmental hazards. Protect chrysalises from predators and pests by using protective enclosures or netting, and handle them with care to avoid causing injury or stress. If damage occurs, assess the severity and provide supportive care as needed to minimize negative impacts on emergence.

By troubleshooting chrysalis issues promptly and effectively, observers can increase the likelihood of successful emergence and support the health and well-being of butterflies and moths. By addressing problems early and implementing appropriate interventions, observers can ensure a smooth transition from pupa to adult insect and contribute to the conservation and enjoyment of these fascinating creatures.

Enhancing Chrysalis Security Measures

Enhancing chrysalis security measures is crucial for protecting pupae from predation, parasitism, and environmental hazards during the vulnerable pupation stage. By implementing proactive strategies to safeguard chrysalises, observers can increase the likelihood of successful emergence and support the health and well-being of developing butterflies and moths.

Here are some effective ways to enhance chrysalis security measures:

1. Use Protective Enclosures: Place chrysalises inside protective enclosures or netted cages to create a physical barrier against predators and pests. Choose enclosures with fine mesh or netting to prevent entry by insects, birds, or other animals while allowing adequate airflow and light penetration.

2. Position Chrysalises Strategically: Select pupation sites that are sheltered, hidden, and inaccessible to potential predators. Place chrysalises in locations such as under leaves, within dense vegetation, or on elevated surfaces out of reach of ground-dwelling predators to minimize the risk of predation or disturbance.

3. Monitor Chrysalis Sites: Regularly monitor chrysalis sites for signs of predation, parasitism, or environmental hazards. Check chrysalises for damage, disturbances, or unusual behavior, and take appropriate action to address any issues promptly.

4. Provide Natural Camouflage: Mimic natural camouflage by placing chrysalises on surfaces that match their coloration and texture, making them less conspicuous to potential predators. Use leaves, branches, or other natural substrates that blend in with the surrounding environment to enhance chrysalis security.

5. Limit Human Intervention: Minimize handling and disturbance of chrysalises to reduce stress and minimize the risk of damage or premature emergence. Avoid unnecessary touching, moving, or manipulation of chrysalises, and provide a quiet and undisturbed environment for pupal development.

By enhancing chrysalis security measures, observers can create a safer and more supportive environment for pupae, promoting successful emergence and contributing to the conservation of butterflies and moths. Through proactive management and vigilant monitoring, observers can help protect chrysalises from threats and ensure the continuation of these fascinating life cycles in the wild.

Promoting Chrysalis Stability and Success

Promoting chrysalis stability and success is essential for ensuring the successful development and emergence of butterflies and moths. Chrysalises are delicate structures that require optimal conditions and careful management to support pupal development and facilitate the transformation from pupa to adult insect.

Here are some effective strategies for promoting chrysalis stability and success:

1. **Provide Secure Pupation Sites:** Select secure pupation sites that offer protection from predators, pests, and environmental hazards. Choose locations that are sheltered, hidden, and inaccessible to potential threats, such as under leaves, within dense vegetation, or on elevated surfaces.

2. **Maintain Stable Environmental Conditions:** Monitor and maintain stable environmental conditions, including temperature, humidity, and lighting levels, to

create a supportive microclimate for chrysalis development. Provide optimal temperature and humidity levels within the chrysalis care environment, and minimize fluctuations that could disrupt pupal development.

3. Ensure Proper Ventilation: Ensure adequate ventilation within the chrysalis care enclosure to prevent the buildup of excess moisture and reduce the risk of fungal or bacterial growth. Use mesh cages or netted enclosures with breathable materials to allow for airflow while maintaining humidity levels.

4. Minimize Disturbance: Minimize handling and disturbance of chrysalises to reduce stress and minimize the risk of damage or premature emergence. Avoid unnecessary touching, moving, or manipulation of chrysalises, and provide a quiet and undisturbed environment for pupal development.

5. Monitor and Respond to Issues: Regularly monitor chrysalis sites for signs of predation, parasitism, or environmental stressors, and take prompt action to address any issues that arise. Remove predators or pests from chrysalis sites, provide supportive care for damaged or stressed pupae, and make adjustments to environmental conditions as needed.

By promoting chrysalis stability and success through careful management and attentive care, observers can increase the likelihood of successful emergence and support the health and well-being of developing butterflies and moths. Through proactive measures and vigilant monitoring, observers can contribute to the conservation and enjoyment of these fascinating insects in the wild.

WITNESSING THE MIRACLE: EMERGENCE OF THE BUTTERFLY

Observing Butterfly Emergence Behaviors

Observing butterfly emergence behaviors is a fascinating and rewarding experience that offers valuable insights into the final stages of metamorphosis and the transition from pupa to adult butterfly. By carefully observing the behaviors exhibited by emerging butterflies, observers can gain a deeper understanding of the process of emergence and appreciate the remarkable transformations taking place before their eyes.

Here are some key behaviors to observe during butterfly emergence:

1. Restlessness: Prior to emergence, the pupa may become restless and exhibit increased movement or agitation within the chrysalis. This restlessness is often a sign that the butterfly is preparing to emerge and may indicate imminent emergence within the next few hours or days.

2. Darkening of Chrysalis: As emergence approaches, the chrysalis may darken or become translucent, allowing observers to see the developing butterfly inside. Look for changes in coloration or texture of the chrysalis, which may indicate that emergence is imminent.

3. Wing Expansion: Upon emerging from the chrysalis, the butterfly will typically hang upside down or cling to its pupal case while it expands and straightens its wings. Observe the gradual unfolding of the wings as they unfurl from the tightly packed pupal structure, forming delicate and intricate patterns.

4. Abdominal Pulsations: During wing expansion, the butterfly may exhibit rhythmic abdominal pulsations or contractions. These movements help pump hemolymph (insect blood) into the wings, causing them to expand and harden into their final shape.

5. Drying Wings: After wing expansion is complete, the butterfly will spend several hours or more drying its wings in preparation for flight. Observe the butterfly as it hangs upside down or perches on a nearby surface, gently fluttering its wings to remove excess moisture and promote drying.

6. Flight Preparation: As the butterfly's wings dry and harden, it will begin to test its flight muscles by flexing and fluttering its wings. Watch for signs of readiness as the butterfly prepares to take its first flight, such as increased wing movement or exploration of its surroundings.

By observing these behaviors closely and attentively, observers can witness the extraordinary process of butterfly emergence and gain a deeper appreciation for the beauty and complexity of nature's life cycles. Through patient observation and careful attention to detail, observers can capture the magic of butterfly emergence and contribute to our understanding of these remarkable insects.

Assisting Butterflies During Emergence

Assisting butterflies during emergence is a delicate process that requires patience, care, and a deep understanding of the butterfly's needs. While it's generally best to allow butterflies to emerge naturally without interference, there are situations where intervention may be necessary to ensure the butterfly's safety and well-being.

Here are some ways to assist butterflies during emergence:

1. Provide a Stable Surface: Ensure that emerging butterflies have a stable surface to cling to while they expand and dry their wings. Use a clean twig, branch, or artificial perch placed near the chrysalis to provide a suitable landing spot for the butterfly.

2. Remove Obstacles: Clear away any obstacles or debris that may obstruct the butterfly's path to freedom. Remove leaves, twigs, or other objects that could impede the butterfly's movement or cause damage to its wings during emergence.

3. Support Wing Expansion: If a butterfly is struggling to expand its wings properly, gently support the wings by carefully lifting them with your fingers. Be cautious not to apply too much pressure or force, as this could cause damage to the delicate wing structures.

4. Provide Shelter: If the weather is inclement or temperatures are too cold for the butterfly to emerge safely, consider providing shelter by moving the chrysalis to a warmer or more protected location. Avoid direct sunlight, strong winds, or extreme temperatures that could stress or harm the emerging butterfly.

5. Monitor Progress: Keep a close eye on the butterfly's progress during emergence, observing its behavior and movement patterns. Be prepared to intervene if the butterfly encounters difficulties or appears to be in distress.

6. Release Safely: Once the butterfly has fully emerged and its wings have dried and hardened, release it into a suitable outdoor habitat. Choose a calm, sunny day with mild temperatures for optimal butterfly release conditions.

By assisting butterflies during emergence with care and sensitivity, observers can help ensure the successful transition from pupa to adult insect and support the health and well-being of these remarkable creatures.

Allowing Butterflies to Dry and Harden Wings

Allowing butterflies to dry and harden their wings is a crucial step in the emergence process that ensures they are fully prepared for flight and survival in their natural habitat. After emerging from their chrysalises, butterflies must undergo a period of wing drying and hardening to attain the strength, flexibility, and stability required for flight.

Here's why allowing butterflies to dry and harden their wings is essential:

1. Wing Expansion: Upon emerging from the chrysalis, butterflies' wings are initially soft, wrinkled, and folded against their bodies. They must undergo a process of expansion to unfurl and stretch their wings to their full size and shape. This expansion is facilitated by the influx of hemolymph (insect blood) into the wing veins, causing them to swell and extend.

2. Removal of Excess Fluid: As butterflies expand their wings, excess fluid is expelled from the wing veins, allowing them to take on a more rigid and structured form. This process helps eliminate excess weight and ensures that the wings achieve the proper balance of strength and flexibility required for flight.

3. Hardening of Wing Scales: As the wings dry, the scales covering the wing surface adhere together, forming a protective layer that strengthens and reinforces the wings. Wing scales provide insulation, waterproofing, and aerodynamic properties essential for flight and survival in the butterfly's environment.

4. Prevention of Wing Damage: Allowing butterflies to dry and harden their wings in a safe and undisturbed environment minimizes the risk of wing damage or deformities that could impair their ability to fly and evade predators. Disturbance or premature handling during the wing-drying process can disrupt the delicate wing structures and compromise the butterfly's chances of survival.

5. Preparation for Flight: Once their wings have fully dried and hardened, butterflies are ready to take their first flight in search of food, mates, and suitable habitat. Strong, well-developed wings are essential for butterflies' survival, enabling them to navigate complex landscapes, evade predators, and fulfill their ecological roles as pollinators and prey items.

By allowing butterflies to dry and harden their wings undisturbed, observers can contribute to the successful emergence and survival of these beautiful insects, ensuring they are well-equipped for the challenges of life in the wild. Patience and respect for the natural process of wing drying and hardening are essential for supporting the health and well-being of butterflies and promoting their conservation in natural ecosystems.

Releasing Butterflies Responsibly

Releasing butterflies responsibly is a thoughtful and considerate act that ensures the well-being and survival of these delicate creatures in their natural habitat. Whether releasing butterflies as part of a conservation effort, educational activity, or celebratory event, it's important to follow guidelines and best practices to minimize stress and maximize their chances of success.

Here are some key principles for releasing butterflies responsibly:

1. Choose a Suitable Release Site: Select a release site that provides appropriate habitat and resources for butterflies, such as nectar-rich flowers, shelter, and suitable microclimates. Avoid releasing butterflies in areas with heavy pesticide use, intense urbanization, or other environmental hazards that could threaten their survival.

2. Consider Weather Conditions: Choose a day with favorable weather conditions for butterfly release, such as mild temperatures, low wind speeds, and clear skies. Avoid releasing butterflies during periods of extreme heat, cold, rain, or strong winds, as these conditions can stress or harm the butterflies and reduce their chances of survival.

3. Release at the Right Time: Release butterflies during the appropriate time of day when they are most active and likely to explore their new surroundings. Early morning or late afternoon are optimal times for butterfly release, as temperatures are cooler and butterflies are more active.

4. Handle with Care: Handle butterflies gently and with care to minimize stress and prevent damage to their delicate wings. Hold butterflies by their wings or thorax with light pressure and avoid touching their wing scales, which are essential for flight and protection.

5. Observe Release Protocol: Follow any specific release protocols or instructions provided by conservation organizations, event organizers, or butterfly suppliers. Some species may require special considerations or restrictions for release, such as quarantine periods or monitoring requirements.

6. Document the Release: Document the butterfly release experience through photography, video, or journaling to commemorate the event and raise awareness about butterfly conservation. Share your observations and experiences with others to inspire appreciation for these beautiful insects and promote conservation efforts.

By releasing butterflies responsibly, observers can contribute to the conservation of butterfly populations and ecosystems, promote public awareness and appreciation for these remarkable insects, and support their continued presence in the natural world. Through thoughtful and considerate actions, we can ensure that butterflies are given the best possible chance to thrive and fulfill their ecological roles as pollinators, prey items, and indicators of environmental health.

Capturing Moments of Butterfly Freedom

Capturing moments of butterfly freedom is a deeply moving and rewarding experience that allows observers to witness the culmination of a remarkable journey from chrysalis to adult butterfly. These fleeting moments represent the culmination of weeks or even months of patience, care, and anticipation, as butterflies emerge from their pupal cases and take flight for the first time.

Here's why capturing these moments is so meaningful:

1. Symbol of Transformation: The moment of butterfly emergence symbolizes the transformative power of nature and the beauty of life's cycles. It serves as a powerful reminder of the incredible metamorphosis that butterflies undergo, from humble caterpillars to graceful winged creatures.

2. Celebration of Freedom: Witnessing a butterfly take flight for the first time is a celebration of freedom and liberation. After being confined within the confines of a chrysalis, butterflies spread their wings and embrace the boundless possibilities of the world around them.

3. Connection with Nature: Capturing moments of butterfly freedom fosters a deeper connection with the natural world and its inhabitants. Observers are reminded of the interconnectedness of all living things and the importance of preserving biodiversity and ecosystems.

4. Sense of Wonder: The sight of a butterfly emerging from its chrysalis and unfurling its wings evokes a sense of wonder and awe. It's a moment of pure magic and beauty that inspires curiosity, appreciation, and reverence for the mysteries of the natural world.

5. Opportunity for Reflection: Capturing moments of butterfly freedom provides an opportunity for reflection and introspection. Observers may contemplate the significance of the moment, reflect on their own journey of growth and transformation, and find inspiration in the resilience and adaptability of butterflies.

6. Sharing and Inspiration: Sharing photos, videos, or stories of butterfly emergence can inspire others to connect with nature, appreciate its wonders, and take action to protect and conserve butterfly habitats. These moments of beauty and freedom have the power to inspire positive change and foster a deeper appreciation for the world around us.

In capturing moments of butterfly freedom, observers not only document a fleeting and precious event but also celebrate the inherent beauty and resilience of life itself. These moments serve as a testament to the power of transformation, the joy of liberation, and the boundless wonder of the natural world.

PROVIDING PROPER NUTRITION FOR ADULT MONARCHS

Understanding monarch butterfly feeding habits is essential for appreciating their ecological role as pollinators and for supporting their conservation efforts. Monarch butterflies undergo a remarkable migration journey and rely on specific plant species for nectar and host plants for egg-laying.

Here's a closer look at monarch butterfly feeding habits:

1. Nectar Feeding: Monarch butterflies primarily feed on the nectar of flowers, which provides them with essential nutrients, energy, and hydration. Monarchs have a preference for flowers with deep tubular shapes, such as milkweed, goldenrod, asters, and coneflowers. They use their long proboscis, a specialized mouthpart, to extract nectar from the flowers' floral tubes.

2. Host Plant Selection: Female monarch butterflies are selective about the plants they choose to lay their eggs on, as monarch caterpillars rely exclusively on milkweed plants (Asclepias spp.) as their host plants. Milkweed serves as the sole food source for monarch caterpillars, providing them with the nutrients and toxins necessary for growth, development, and defense against predators.

3. Migration Feeding Stations: During their long-distance migration, monarch butterflies rely on a network of nectar-rich feeding stations to refuel and replenish their energy reserves. These feeding stations, often located along migratory routes or in overwintering sites, provide essential resources for monarchs to survive their arduous journey.

4. Seasonal Variation: Monarch butterfly feeding habits exhibit seasonal variation, with fluctuations in nectar availability and plant phenology influencing their foraging behavior. In the spring and summer months, monarchs actively seek out flowering plants for nectar and milkweed for egg-laying. During the fall migration and overwintering periods, monarchs rely on specific nectar sources to sustain them during periods of reduced activity.

5. Conservation Importance: Understanding monarch butterfly feeding habits is critical for designing effective conservation strategies to support their populations. Protecting and restoring habitat areas with diverse plant species and maintaining nectar-rich flower patches along migratory routes are essential for ensuring the availability of food resources for monarch butterflies throughout their life cycle.

By understanding monarch butterfly feeding habits and the plant species they rely on, we can take proactive measures to conserve and protect their habitats, promote pollinator-friendly landscapes, and contribute to the preservation of these iconic insects for future generations.

Creating Butterfly Feeding Stations

Creating butterfly feeding stations is a wonderful way to support the health and well-being of butterflies while enhancing the beauty and biodiversity of your outdoor space. These feeding stations provide essential nectar resources for butterflies, serving as refueling stations for adults and supporting their survival and reproductive success.

Here's how to create butterfly feeding stations:

1. Select Butterfly-Friendly Plants: Choose a variety of flowering plants that are attractive to butterflies and provide abundant nectar. Opt for native plant species whenever possible, as they are well-adapted to local environmental conditions and support native butterfly species. Some excellent nectar plants for butterflies include milkweed, coneflowers, butterfly bush, asters, and verbena.

2. Plan for Continuous Bloom: Select plants with staggered bloom times to ensure a continuous supply of nectar throughout the growing season. By incorporating early, mid, and late-blooming flowers into your butterfly garden, you can provide nectar resources for butterflies from spring through fall, supporting their needs during different life stages and migration periods.

3. Provide Sunlight and Shelter: Place butterfly feeding stations in sunny, sheltered locations with ample sunlight and protection from strong winds. Butterflies are ectothermic organisms and rely on sunlight to regulate their body temperature and energy levels.

Additionally, provide sheltered areas such as shrubs or trees where butterflies can rest and seek refuge from predators and adverse weather conditions.

4. Include Water Sources: Incorporate shallow dishes or saucers filled with clean water to provide drinking opportunities for butterflies. Butterflies require hydration, especially during hot weather or drought conditions. Adding rocks or pebbles to the water source provides landing pads for butterflies to perch while drinking.

5. Avoid using chemical pesticides and herbicides in your butterfly garden, as these substances can harm butterflies, caterpillars, and other beneficial insects. Instead, opt for organic gardening practices and natural pest control methods to maintain a healthy and balanced ecosystem.

6. Regularly maintain your butterfly feeding stations by watering, weeding, and deadheading spent flowers to encourage continuous bloom. Monitor the garden for signs of butterfly activity, such as nectaring, egg-laying,

and caterpillar feeding, and make adjustments as needed to optimize habitat conditions.

Creating butterfly feeding stations not only benefits butterflies but also provides a rewarding and educational experience for gardeners of all ages. By cultivating a welcoming habitat with abundant nectar resources, you can attract a diverse array of butterfly species to your garden and contribute to their conservation and enjoyment for years to come.

Offering Nutritious Nectar Sources

Offering nutritious nectar sources is essential for supporting the health and vitality of butterflies, providing them with the energy and nutrients they need for flight, reproduction, and overall survival. Nectar is the primary food source for adult butterflies, supplying them with carbohydrates, sugars, and other essential nutrients.

1. Choose Nectar-Rich Plants: Select a variety of flowering plants that are attractive to butterflies and provide abundant nectar. Opt for native plant species whenever possible, as they are well-adapted to local environmental conditions and support native butterfly species. Some excellent nectar plants for butterflies include milkweed, coneflowers, butterfly bush, asters, and verbena.

2. Plan for Continuous Bloom: Select plants with staggered bloom times to ensure a continuous supply of nectar throughout the growing season. By incorporating early, mid, and late-blooming flowers into your garden, you can provide nectar resources for butterflies from spring through fall, supporting their needs during different life stages and migration periods.

3. Provide a Variety of Flower Shapes: Offer flowers with diverse shapes, sizes, and colors to attract a wide range of butterfly species. Butterflies have different preferences for nectar sources, with some species favoring deep tubular flowers and others preferring flat or open blooms. Including a variety of flower shapes ensures that you cater to the needs of different butterfly species.

4. Avoid Chemical Pesticides: Refrain from using chemical pesticides and herbicides in your garden, as these substances can harm butterflies, caterpillars, and other beneficial insects. Instead, opt for organic gardening practices and natural pest control methods to maintain a healthy and balanced ecosystem.

5. Provide Water Sources: Offer shallow dishes or saucers filled with clean water to provide drinking opportunities for butterflies. Butterflies require hydration, especially during hot weather or drought conditions. Adding rocks or pebbles to the water source provides landing pads for butterflies to perch while drinking.

By offering nutritious nectar sources in your garden, you can attract a diverse array of butterfly species and provide them with the essential resources they need to thrive. Creating a welcoming habitat with abundant nectar plants not only benefits butterflies but also enhances the beauty and biodiversity of your outdoor space.

Maintaining Feeding Stations Cleanliness

Maintaining feeding stations cleanliness is essential for ensuring the health and well-being of butterflies and other pollinators that rely on these resources for nourishment. Clean feeding stations reduce the risk of contamination, disease transmission, and insect infestations, creating a safe and hygienic environment for butterflies to feed and thrive.

Here are some tips for maintaining feeding stations cleanliness:

1. Regular Cleaning: Establish a regular cleaning schedule for your feeding stations, aiming to clean them at least once a week or as needed. Remove any debris, fallen flowers, or dead insects from the feeding station to prevent accumulation and contamination.

2. Replace Nectar Regularly: If you provide artificial nectar solutions for butterflies, such as sugar water or commercial nectar mixes, be sure to replace the nectar regularly to prevent spoilage and bacterial growth. Change the nectar solution every 2-3 days, or sooner if it becomes cloudy or discolored.

3. Clean Water Sources: If you offer water sources for butterflies to drink from, such as shallow dishes or saucers, be sure to clean and refill them regularly to prevent stagnation and mosquito breeding. Empty and clean water sources every few days, and replace them with fresh, clean water to ensure hydration for butterflies.

4. Avoid Mold and Mildew: Check feeding stations for signs of mold or mildew growth, especially in humid or damp conditions. Cleanse feeding stations with mild soap and water, vinegar solution, or hydrogen peroxide to remove any fungal or bacterial growth and inhibit further contamination.

5. Monitor for Pests: Regularly inspect feeding stations for signs of pest infestations, such as ants, bees, or wasps. If pests are present, take steps to deter or remove them from the feeding area using natural repellents or physical barriers.

6. Maintain Surrounding Area: Keep the surrounding area of feeding stations clean and free from debris, weeds, and standing water that could attract pests or harbor pathogens. Prune vegetation, remove fallen leaves, and maintain a tidy garden environment to promote cleanliness and hygiene.

By maintaining feeding stations cleanliness, observers can create a healthy and inviting environment for butterflies to feed and thrive. Clean feeding stations reduce the risk of disease transmission and contamination, ensuring that butterflies have access to safe and nutritious food sources to support their health and well-being. Through regular cleaning and monitoring, observers can contribute to the conservation of butterfly populations and promote a vibrant and biodiverse ecosystem in their gardens.

Supplementing Adult Monarch Diets When Necessary

Supplementing adult monarch diets when necessary is a proactive measure to support their health and vitality, especially during times of nectar scarcity or environmental stress. Monarch butterflies rely heavily on nectar as their primary food source, and fluctuations in nectar availability due to factors such as habitat loss, weather conditions, and seasonal variations can impact their ability to find sufficient nourishment.

Here's why supplementing adult monarch diets is important and how it can be done effectively:

1. Addressing Nectar Scarcity: In regions where nectar-rich flowering plants are scarce or during periods of drought or extreme weather, adult monarchs may struggle to find enough food to sustain themselves. Supplementing their diets with additional nectar sources ensures that they have access to the energy and nutrients they need for flight, reproduction, and survival.

2. Promoting Health and Longevity: Providing supplemental nectar sources can help maintain the health and longevity of adult monarchs, reducing the risk of starvation, dehydration, and weakened immune systems. By ensuring that butterflies are well-nourished, observers can support their ability to withstand environmental challenges and successfully complete their life cycle.

3. Enhancing Reproductive Success: Adult monarchs require sufficient energy reserves to support egg production and mating activities. Supplemental nectar sources provide the fuel needed for females to lay eggs and males to engage in courtship behaviors, increasing the likelihood of successful reproduction and offspring survival.

4. Offering Nectar-Rich Flowers: Supplement adult monarch diets by planting nectar-rich flowers in butterfly gardens, parks, and other suitable habitats. Choose a variety of flowering plants with staggered bloom times to provide a continuous supply of nectar throughout the growing season. Opt for native plant species whenever possible, as they are well-adapted to local environmental conditions and support native butterfly species.

5. Providing Artificial Nectar Solutions: Offer artificial nectar solutions, such as sugar water or commercial nectar mixes, in shallow dishes or feeders placed in butterfly gardens or outdoor spaces. Mix one part sugar with four parts water to create a homemade nectar solution that mimics the natural nectar composition of flowers.

6. Maintaining Cleanliness and Hygiene: Regularly clean and replenish supplemental nectar sources to prevent spoilage, contamination, and insect infestations. Change sugar water or commercial nectar solutions every 2-3 days, and clean feeding stations with mild soap and water to remove debris and inhibit bacterial growth.

By supplementing adult monarch diets when necessary, observers can help mitigate the impacts of nectar scarcity and support the health and survival of these iconic butterflies. Through thoughtful and proactive measures, we can ensure that monarchs have access to the resources they need to thrive and continue their remarkable migration journey for generations to come.

ENSURING SAFE RELEASE AND MIGRATION

Timing Releases for Optimal Migration Periods

Timing releases for optimal migration periods is crucial for maximizing the chances of success and survival for monarch butterflies as they embark on their remarkable journey. Monarch butterflies undergo a spectacular migration from their summer breeding grounds in North America to overwintering sites in Mexico or California, covering thousands of miles in search of suitable habitat and resources.

**Here's why timing releases for optimal migration periods is important and how it can be achieved effectively:**

1. Maximizing Weather Conditions: Timing releases to coincide with favorable weather conditions is essential for ensuring the safety and success of migrating monarchs. Ideal weather conditions for migration include mild temperatures, clear skies, and gentle winds, which facilitate long-distance flight and reduce the risk of exposure to extreme weather events such as storms or high winds.

2. Utilizing Environmental Cues: Monarch butterflies use environmental cues such as day length, temperature, and availability of resources to regulate their migratory behavior. Timing releases to align with natural cues and seasonal patterns ensures that butterflies are in sync with optimal migration periods and can navigate their way to overwintering sites successfully.

3. Avoiding Premature Releases: Releasing monarch butterflies too early in the season or before they have built up sufficient energy reserves can result in premature migration attempts and increased vulnerability to environmental hazards. It's essential to wait until conditions are conducive to migration and butterflies are well-prepared for the journey before releasing them into the wild.

4. Monitoring Migration Patterns: Monitoring regional migration patterns and tracking the movement of monarch populations can help determine the optimal timing for releases in specific geographic areas. By staying informed about the progress of the migration and local conditions, observers can make informed decisions about when and where to release monarch butterflies for optimal results.

5. Coordinating with Conservation Efforts: Coordinate releases with ongoing conservation efforts and community-based monarch conservation initiatives to maximize the impact and effectiveness of release events. Participating in coordinated release programs allows observers to contribute to larger-scale conservation efforts and support the conservation of monarch butterflies and their habitats.

By timing releases for optimal migration periods, observers can help ensure the success and survival of monarch butterflies as they undertake their epic migration journey. Through strategic planning, coordination, and attention to environmental factors, we can support the conservation of these iconic insects and contribute to their continued presence in the natural world.

Selecting Suitable Release Sites

Selecting suitable release sites is crucial for ensuring the success and well-being of released butterflies, providing them with access to suitable habitat, resources, and environmental conditions necessary for survival. When choosing release sites, several factors should be considered to maximize the effectiveness and impact of release events.

Here's how to select suitable release sites:

1. Habitat Suitability: Choose release sites with suitable habitat characteristics that are conducive to butterfly survival and reproduction. Look for areas with abundant nectar-rich flowers, host plants for caterpillars, and sheltered resting spots such as trees, shrubs, or dense vegetation. Avoid releasing butterflies in areas with limited habitat diversity, high levels of pollution, or heavy pesticide use.

2. Native Plant Availability: Select release sites that support native plant species preferred by butterflies for nectar and host plants. Native plants are well-adapted to local environmental conditions and provide essential resources for butterflies throughout their life cycle. Incorporate a diverse range of native plant species into release sites to ensure a continuous supply of food and shelter for released butterflies.

3. Accessibility: Choose release sites that are easily accessible to released butterflies and observers, allowing for safe and convenient release activities. Select locations with ample space for butterflies to disperse and explore their surroundings without encountering obstacles or hazards. Consider factors such as parking, trails, and amenities when selecting release sites for public or educational events.

4. Environmental Conditions: Consider environmental factors such as sunlight, temperature, humidity, and wind exposure when selecting release sites. Choose sites with moderate temperatures, gentle breezes, and suitable microclimates that support butterfly activity and flight. Avoid releasing butterflies during extreme weather conditions such as high winds, heavy rain, or extreme heat.

5. Conservation Priorities: Align release activities with local conservation priorities and initiatives aimed at supporting butterfly populations and habitat restoration efforts. Choose release sites that contribute to broader conservation goals, such as promoting biodiversity, enhancing pollinator habitat, or restoring native ecosystems.

By carefully selecting suitable release sites, observers can maximize the effectiveness and impact of release events, ensuring the success and survival of released butterflies in their new environment. Through thoughtful planning, consideration of habitat characteristics, and alignment with conservation priorities, we can support the conservation of butterfly populations and promote their continued presence in the natural world.

Releasing Butterflies with Care and Respect

Releasing butterflies with care and respect is a meaningful and thoughtful practice that honors the beauty and significance of these delicate creatures. Whether releasing butterflies for conservation, education, or celebratory purposes, it's essential to approach the process with sensitivity and mindfulness to ensure the well-being and success of the released butterflies.

Here's how to release butterflies with care and respect:

1. Handle with Gentleness: Handle butterflies gently and with care, avoiding excessive touching or handling that could damage their delicate wings or cause stress. Hold butterflies by their wings or thorax with light pressure, being mindful not to pinch or squeeze them.

2. Provide a Suitable Environment: Choose a release site with suitable habitat characteristics, including abundant nectar-rich flowers, host plants, and sheltered resting spots. Ensure that the release site is free from hazards such as predators, pollutants, and extreme weather conditions that could threaten the safety of released butterflies.

3. Release at the Right Time: Release butterflies during the appropriate time of day when they are most active and likely to explore their new surroundings. Early morning or late afternoon are optimal times for butterfly release, as temperatures are cooler and butterflies are more active.

4. Observe Release Protocol: Follow any specific release protocols or instructions provided by conservation organizations, event organizers, or butterfly suppliers. Some species may require special considerations or restrictions for release, such as quarantine periods or monitoring requirements.

5. Promote Awareness: Use butterfly release events as opportunities to raise awareness about butterfly conservation, habitat protection, and the importance of preserving biodiversity. Educate participants about the life cycle of butterflies, their ecological roles, and the threats they face in the wild.

6. Document and Reflect: Document the butterfly release experience through photography, video, or journaling to commemorate the event and reflect on its significance. Take a moment to observe the released butterflies as they take flight and embark on their journey, appreciating their beauty and symbolism.

By releasing butterflies with care and respect, observers can honor the inherent value of these remarkable insects and contribute to their conservation and preservation in the natural world. Through mindful and thoughtful actions, we can ensure that released butterflies have the best possible chance to thrive and fulfill their ecological roles as pollinators, prey items, and indicators of environmental health.

Monitoring Released Butterflies in the Wild

Monitoring released butterflies in the wild is a valuable practice that provides insights into their behavior, habitat preferences, and overall success following release. By carefully observing released butterflies and documenting their activities, researchers, conservationists, and enthusiasts can gain valuable information about population dynamics, migration patterns, and the effectiveness of release efforts.

Here's why monitoring released butterflies is important and how it can be done effectively:

1. Assessing Survival and Adaptation: Monitoring released butterflies allows observers to assess their survival rates and ability to adapt to their new environment. By tracking individual butterflies over time, researchers can determine whether released individuals successfully integrate into the wild population and establish themselves in suitable habitat.

2. Gathering Behavioral Data: Observing released butterflies in the wild provides valuable insights into their behavior, including foraging preferences, mating behaviors, and territorial interactions. By documenting behavioral observations, researchers can gain a better understanding of butterfly ecology and inform conservation strategies.

3. Evaluating Habitat Suitability: Monitoring released butterflies helps evaluate the suitability of release sites and habitat conditions for supporting butterfly populations. By assessing factors such as nectar availability, host plant abundance, and habitat connectivity, observers can identify areas that provide optimal resources for butterfly survival and reproduction.

4. Detecting Threats and Challenges: Monitoring released butterflies enables observers to detect potential threats and challenges facing butterfly populations, such as habitat loss, predation, disease, and climate change. By identifying and addressing these threats early, conservation efforts can be targeted more effectively to mitigate negative impacts on butterfly populations.

5. Contributing to Research and Conservation: Data collected from monitoring released butterflies contributes to scientific research and conservation initiatives aimed at protecting butterfly populations and their habitats. By sharing observations and findings with the broader scientific community, observers can contribute to our understanding of butterfly ecology and inform conservation decision-making.

6. Engaging Citizen Scientists: Involving citizen scientists in butterfly monitoring efforts encourages public participation in conservation and fosters a sense of stewardship for the natural world. Citizen scientists can contribute valuable data through butterfly counts, observations, and reporting, expanding the reach and impact of monitoring efforts.

By monitoring released butterflies in the wild, observers can gain valuable insights into butterfly ecology, behavior, and conservation needs, contributing to the protection and preservation of these iconic insects for future generations. Through careful observation, documentation, and collaboration, we can ensure the long-term survival and sustainability of butterfly populations in their natural habitats.

Contributing to Citizen Science Initiatives

Contributing to citizen science initiatives is a meaningful way for individuals to actively participate in scientific research, conservation efforts, and environmental monitoring. Citizen science harnesses the collective power of volunteers to collect data, conduct research, and address complex scientific challenges, often involving collaboration between scientists, educators, and the public.

Here's why contributing to citizen science initiatives is important and how individuals can get involved:

1. Advancing Scientific Knowledge: Citizen science enables participants to contribute valuable data and observations that contribute to scientific research and discovery. By engaging in data collection, monitoring, and analysis, citizen scientists help expand our understanding of biodiversity, ecology, climate change, and other scientific topics.

2. Supporting Conservation Efforts: Citizen science plays a critical role in conservation by providing information on species distributions, population trends, and habitat conditions. By monitoring wildlife populations, tracking invasive species, and assessing habitat quality, citizen scientists help inform conservation strategies and protect vulnerable ecosystems.

3. Empowering Public Engagement: Citizen science empowers individuals to actively engage with scientific inquiry and environmental issues, fostering a sense of curiosity, discovery, and stewardship for the natural world. By participating in hands-on research activities, citizen scientists develop a deeper appreciation for science and become advocates for conservation and environmental sustainability.

4. Informing Policy and Management: Data collected through citizen science initiatives can inform decision-making processes, policy development, and natural resource management. By providing policymakers and land managers with reliable, up-to-date information, citizen scientists contribute to evidence-based decision-making and promote more effective conservation and management practices.

5. Promoting Education and Outreach: Citizen science initiatives provide educational opportunities for participants of all ages to learn about scientific methods, ecological principles, and environmental issues. By engaging in citizen science projects, individuals gain hands-on experience in scientific inquiry and develop critical thinking, problem-solving, and communication skills.

6. Building Community Connections: Citizen science fosters collaboration and community engagement by bringing together scientists, educators, policymakers, and the public to work towards common goals. By participating in citizen science initiatives, individuals connect with like-minded individuals, build networks, and contribute to collective efforts to address pressing environmental challenges.

By contributing to citizen science initiatives, individuals can make meaningful contributions to scientific research, conservation efforts, and environmental stewardship. Whether through data collection, monitoring, advocacy, or outreach, citizen scientists play a vital role in advancing our understanding of the natural world and promoting sustainable solutions for the benefit of people and planet.

ENGAGING IN MONARCH CONSERVATION EFFORTS

Participating in Monarch Tagging Programs

Participating in monarch tagging programs is a meaningful way for individuals to contribute to scientific research and conservation efforts aimed at understanding monarch butterfly migration patterns, population dynamics, and habitat needs. Monarch tagging involves attaching small, lightweight tags to the wings of monarch butterflies to track their movements and monitor their populations.

Here's why participating in monarch tagging programs is important and how individuals can get involved:

1. Tracking Migration Routes: Monarch tagging programs help researchers track the migratory movements of monarch butterflies as they travel thousands of miles between their breeding grounds in North America and overwintering sites in Mexico or California. By tagging monarchs at various locations and recording tag recoveries, researchers can map migration routes, timing, and destinations to better understand the factors influencing monarch migration.

2. Monitoring Population Trends: Tagging monarch butterflies provides valuable data on population trends, abundance, and distribution across different regions and habitats. By monitoring tagged individuals over time, researchers can assess population dynamics, population size, and fluctuations in response to environmental changes, habitat loss, and other threats.

3. Engaging Citizen Scientists: Monarch tagging programs engage citizen scientists of all ages and backgrounds in hands-on research and conservation activities. Participants learn about monarch biology, ecology, and migration while contributing to scientific knowledge and conservation efforts. Tagging events, workshops, and educational materials provide opportunities for public involvement and awareness-raising.

4. Supporting Conservation Initiatives: Data collected through monarch tagging programs informs conservation initiatives aimed at protecting monarch butterflies and their habitats. By understanding migration patterns, habitat requirements, and population trends, conservationists can implement targeted strategies to conserve critical habitat, restore native plant communities, and mitigate threats to monarch populations.

5. Promoting Collaboration: Monarch tagging programs foster collaboration among researchers, conservation organizations, educators, and the public to address shared goals and challenges. By working together, participants can leverage collective expertise, resources, and networks to advance monarch conservation and promote sustainable solutions.

Participating in monarch tagging programs provides individuals with a unique opportunity to contribute to scientific discovery, conservation action, and the preservation of monarch butterflies for future generations. By tagging monarchs and sharing data, participants play a vital role in protecting one of nature's most iconic and beloved insects.

Advocating for Monarch-Friendly Policies

Advocating for monarch-friendly policies is a crucial step in protecting and preserving monarch butterflies and their habitats, addressing threats such as habitat loss, pesticide use, climate change, and other environmental challenges. By advocating for policies that promote monarch conservation, individuals can influence decision-making at the local, regional, and national levels and drive positive change for monarch populations.

**Here's why advocating for monarch-friendly policies is important and how individuals can make a difference:**

1. Protecting Habitat: Monarch butterflies rely on diverse habitats, including milkweed-rich grasslands, prairies, meadows, and urban green spaces, throughout their life cycle. Advocating for policies that prioritize habitat conservation, restoration, and protection ensures that critical habitat areas are preserved and managed to support monarch populations and promote biodiversity.

2. Reducing Pesticide Use: Pesticides, particularly neonicotinoids and glyphosate-based herbicides, pose significant threats to monarch butterflies and other pollinators. Advocating for policies that restrict or regulate pesticide use, promote integrated pest management practices, and support alternatives to chemical pesticides helps minimize the impact of pesticides on monarch populations and their habitats.

3. Promoting Native Plant Conservation: Native plants, especially milkweed species, are essential for monarch butterflies as they provide food for caterpillars and nectar for adult butterflies. Advocating for policies that prioritize native plant conservation, habitat restoration, and pollinator-friendly landscaping promotes the availability of suitable habitat and resources for monarchs and other pollinators.

4. Addressing Climate Change: Climate change poses a significant threat to monarch butterflies and their migratory habitats, affecting temperature patterns, weather events, and plant phenology. Advocating for policies that address climate change, promote renewable energy sources, reduce greenhouse gas emissions, and support climate-resilient landscapes helps mitigate the impacts of climate change on monarch populations and their habitats.

5. Educating and Mobilizing Communities: Advocating for monarch-friendly policies involves raising awareness, educating policymakers, and mobilizing communities to take action. Individuals can engage in advocacy efforts through letter-writing campaigns, petitions, public forums, and grassroots organizing to voice their support for monarch conservation and influence decision-makers to prioritize monarch-friendly policies.

By advocating for monarch-friendly policies, individuals can contribute to the protection and preservation of monarch butterflies and their habitats, ensuring that these iconic insects continue to inspire and enrich our natural world for generations to come. Through collective action and advocacy, we can create a brighter future for monarchs and foster a healthier environment for all living beings.

Supporting Monarch Habitat Restoration Projects

Supporting monarch habitat restoration projects is a meaningful way for individuals to contribute to the conservation and recovery of monarch butterflies and their habitats. Habitat loss, fragmentation, and degradation are significant threats to monarch populations, making habitat restoration efforts critical for their survival. By getting involved in habitat restoration projects, individuals can help create and restore monarch-friendly habitats, promote biodiversity, and address broader environmental challenges.

1. Providing Essential Habitat: Monarch butterflies rely on diverse habitats, including milkweed-rich grasslands, prairies, meadows, and urban green spaces, throughout their life cycle. Supporting habitat restoration projects helps create and enhance these essential habitats, providing food, shelter, and breeding grounds for monarchs and other pollinators.

2. Promoting Native Plant Conservation: Native plants, especially milkweed species, are essential for monarch butterflies as they provide food for caterpillars and nectar for adult butterflies. Supporting habitat restoration projects that prioritize native plant conservation, habitat restoration, and pollinator-friendly landscaping promotes the availability of suitable habitat and resources for monarchs and other pollinators.

3. Enhancing Biodiversity: Habitat restoration projects contribute to biodiversity conservation by creating and restoring diverse ecosystems that support a wide range of plant and animal species. By restoring native plant communities, improving habitat connectivity, and enhancing ecosystem health, habitat restoration efforts benefit not only monarchs but also other wildlife species and the environment as a whole.

4. Mitigating Environmental Threats: Habitat restoration projects help mitigate environmental threats such as habitat loss, fragmentation, and degradation, which negatively impact monarch populations and their habitats. By restoring degraded habitats, protecting critical habitat areas, and implementing conservation practices, habitat restoration efforts address key threats to monarch butterflies and promote their long-term survival.

5. Engaging Communities: Habitat restoration projects engage communities in hands-on conservation activities, raising awareness, building connections to nature, and fostering a sense of stewardship for the environment. By volunteering, participating in restoration activities, and supporting local conservation organizations, individuals can make a tangible impact on monarch habitat restoration efforts and contribute to a healthier, more sustainable future for monarchs and their habitats.

By supporting monarch habitat restoration projects, individuals can play a vital role in the conservation and recovery of monarch butterflies and their habitats, ensuring that these iconic insects continue to thrive for generations to come. Through collective action and community involvement, we can make a positive difference for monarchs and create a brighter future for biodiversity and the environment.

Educating Others About Monarch Conservation

Educating others about monarch conservation is a powerful and effective way to raise awareness, inspire action, and mobilize support for the protection and preservation of monarch butterflies and their habitats. By sharing knowledge, engaging in outreach activities, and fostering connections to nature, individuals can empower others to become informed advocates and stewards for monarch conservation.

Here's why educating others about monarch conservation is important and how individuals can make a difference:

1. Raising Awareness: Many people are unaware of the challenges facing monarch butterflies and the importance of their conservation. By educating others about the threats to monarch populations, including habitat loss, pesticide use, climate change, and other environmental pressures, individuals can raise awareness and increase understanding of the need for conservation action.

2. Promoting Appreciation: Educating others about the life cycle, behaviors, and ecological significance of monarch butterflies helps foster appreciation and admiration for these iconic insects. By highlighting their remarkable migration journey, intricate biology, and vital role as pollinators, individuals can inspire others to value and protect monarchs and their habitats.

3.   Empowering Action: Education empowers individuals to take meaningful action to support monarch conservation efforts. By providing information about practical steps that individuals can take, such as planting native milkweed and nectar plants, avoiding pesticide use, participating in citizen science projects, and supporting habitat restoration initiatives, educators motivate others to make a positive difference for monarchs.

4. Building Partnerships: Educating others about monarch conservation fosters collaboration and partnerships among diverse stakeholders, including educators, students, conservation organizations, policymakers, and the public. By working together, individuals can leverage collective expertise, resources, and networks to address shared conservation goals and challenges.

5. Fostering a Conservation Ethic: Education instills a sense of responsibility and stewardship for the natural world, encouraging individuals to become active participants in conservation efforts. By nurturing a conservation ethic and promoting environmental literacy, educators cultivate a culture of caring and respect for nature that extends beyond monarchs to benefit biodiversity and the planet as a whole.

By educating others about monarch conservation, individuals can play a vital role in raising awareness, inspiring action, and fostering a deeper connection to nature. Through outreach, advocacy, and engagement, we can empower others to join us in protecting and preserving monarch butterflies for future generations to enjoy and appreciate.

Taking Action to Protect Monarchs for Future Generations

Taking action to protect monarchs for future generations is essential to ensure the continued survival and well-being of these iconic butterflies. With their remarkable migration journey, intricate life cycle, and ecological significance as pollinators, monarch butterflies hold a special place in the natural world. By implementing conservation measures and advocating for monarch-friendly policies, individuals can make a meaningful difference in safeguarding monarch populations for generations to come.

1. Planting Milkweed and Nectar Plants: One of the most effective ways to support monarchs is by planting native milkweed and nectar plants in gardens, parks, and other green spaces. Milkweed serves as the sole host plant for monarch caterpillars, while nectar plants provide essential food sources for adult butterflies. By creating monarch-friendly habitats, individuals can help replenish critical resources and support monarch populations throughout their life cycle.

2. Avoiding Pesticide Use: Pesticides, particularly neonicotinoids and glyphosate-based herbicides, pose significant threats to monarch butterflies and other pollinators. Avoiding the use of chemical pesticides in gardens and landscapes helps protect monarchs from exposure to harmful toxins and preserves their habitat and food sources.

3. Participating in Citizen Science: Get involved in citizen science initiatives focused on monarch monitoring, tagging, and research. By participating in butterfly counts, reporting sightings, and contributing data to scientific databases, individuals can help track monarch populations, migration patterns, and habitat changes, providing valuable insights for conservation efforts.

4. Supporting Habitat Restoration: Volunteer with local conservation organizations and participate in habitat restoration projects aimed at restoring monarch-friendly habitats. By planting native vegetation, removing invasive species, and restoring degraded ecosystems, individuals can create and enhance habitat corridors and breeding grounds for monarchs and other wildlife.

5. Advocating for Policies: Advocate for monarch-friendly policies at the local, state, and national levels to address key threats to monarch populations, including habitat loss, pesticide use, climate change, and urbanization. Support initiatives that prioritize habitat conservation, promote native plant landscaping, and reduce pesticide exposure to create a more monarch-friendly environment for future generations.

By taking action to protect monarchs for future generations, individuals can ensure that these iconic butterflies continue to enchant and inspire people for years to come. Through collective efforts and shared commitment to conservation, we can preserve monarch populations and their extraordinary migration for generations to enjoy and appreciate.

CONCLUSION: BECOMING A STEWARD OF MONARCH BUTTERFLIES

Becoming a steward of monarch butterflies is a rewarding and impactful journey that involves taking proactive steps to protect, conserve, and advocate for these iconic insects. Monarchs face numerous threats to their survival, including habitat loss, pesticide use, climate change, and other environmental pressures. By becoming a steward of monarch butterflies, individuals can play a vital role in ensuring the continued presence and prosperity of these remarkable creatures for future generations to enjoy.

Here's how to become a steward of monarch butterflies:

1. Educate Yourself: Start by learning about monarch butterflies, their life cycle, migration journey, and ecological significance. Understand the challenges facing monarch populations, including habitat loss, pesticide use, climate change, and disease. By educating yourself about monarch biology and conservation issues, you can become better equipped to take informed action and advocate for monarch-friendly policies and practices.

2. Create Monarch-Friendly Habitats: Transform your outdoor space into a monarch-friendly habitat by planting native milkweed and nectar plants. Milkweed serves as the sole host plant for monarch caterpillars, while nectar plants provide essential food sources for adult butterflies. Choose a variety of native plant species with staggered bloom times to provide continuous food sources throughout the growing season. Design your garden to include sheltered resting spots, water sources, and habitat features that cater to the needs of monarchs at different stages of their life cycle.

3. Avoid Pesticide Use: Minimize or eliminate the use of chemical pesticides in your garden and landscaping practices. Pesticides, particularly neonicotinoids and glyphosate-based herbicides, pose significant threats to monarch butterflies and other pollinators. Opt for organic and non-toxic pest control methods, such as handpicking pests, using biological controls, and practicing integrated pest management, to protect monarchs and preserve their habitat.

4. Participate in Citizen Science: Get involved in citizen science initiatives focused on monarch monitoring, tagging, and research. Join butterfly counts, report monarch sightings, and contribute data to scientific databases to help track monarch populations, migration patterns, and habitat changes. By participating in citizen science projects, you can make meaningful contributions to monarch conservation efforts and support scientific research and monitoring efforts.

5. Advocate for Monarch-Friendly Policies: Advocate for policies and regulations that promote monarch conservation and protect their habitats. Support initiatives that prioritize habitat restoration, native plant landscaping, and reduced pesticide use in urban, agricultural, and natural areas. Write letters to policymakers, participate in public hearings, and join advocacy campaigns to voice your support for monarch-friendly policies and practices.

6. Educate Others: Share your knowledge and passion for monarch conservation with others in your community. Organize educational events, workshops, and presentations to raise awareness about monarch butterflies, their ecological importance, and the threats they face. Engage schools, community groups, and local organizations in monarch-related activities and projects to inspire collective action and stewardship.

7. Support Conservation Organizations: Contribute your time, resources, and support to conservation organizations dedicated to monarch butterfly conservation. Volunteer with local conservation groups, participate in habitat restoration projects, and donate to monarch conservation initiatives to help fund research, conservation efforts, and education programs.

By becoming a steward of monarch butterflies, you can make a positive impact on their conservation and help ensure their survival for future generations to enjoy. Through thoughtful action, advocacy, and education, individuals can play a vital role in protecting monarch populations and preserving their extraordinary migration for years to come.